SO

WARRIOR ELITE

A SIX WEEK SPECIAL FORCES CHALLENGE FOR MEN

CODY BOBAY
FOREWORD BY CLIFF GRAHAM

© 2018 by Soulcon Publishing

All rights reserved. No part of this book may be reproduced in any form without the permission in writing from the publisher, except in the case of brief quotations in printed articles or reviews.

ISBN: 9780985667863

Printed in the United States of America

Scripture taken from the New King James Version. Copyright © 1982 by Thomas Nelson, Inc. Used by permission. All rights reserved.

Scriptures taken from the Holy Bible, New International Version®, NIV®. Copyright © 1973, 1978, 1984, 2011 by Biblica, Inc.™ Used by permission of Zondervan. All rights reserved worldwide.

Scripture taken from the NLT are taken from the Holy Bible, New Living Translation, copyright © 1996, 2004, 2007 by Tyndale House Foundation. Used by permission of Tyndale House Publishers, Inc., Carol Stream, Illinois 60188. All rights reserved.

Scripture taken from The Message. Copyright © 1993, 1994, 1995, 1996, 2000, 2001, 2002. Used by permission of NavPress Publishing Group.

TABLE OF CONTENTS

FOREWORD

You may not want to approach this book.

It's not the typical men's ministry volume that makes a few good points and then fades in your memory. It grabs you by the throat, shakes you, punches your chest, slaps you around a bit, and then demands to know if you are still paying attention.

Cody Bobay is a man whose allegiance is captivated by Jesus Christ, and through his leadership, Soulcon is pioneering a raw, aggressive, Gospel-centered transformation system for men that is changing lives all over the world.

You were designed by God to be Warrior Elite. With this resource and the brotherhood that comes with it, you will be physically tired, emotionally drained, and spiritually challenged...and you will never be the same again.

Cliff Graham
Author of the Lion of War Series

DEDICATION

"However, I consider my life worth nothing to me; my only aim is to finish the race and complete the task the Lord Jesus has given me—the task of testifying to the good news of God's grace."

Acts 20:24 (NIV)

I cannot praise God enough for the opportunity to steward the movement of Soulcon on this earth. The Lord knows this brotherhood is what I need to live strong and focused for the Kingdom daily as I walk in the Spirit and not in the flesh. The fact that Jesus died for sinners like you and me, and the way He loves us unconditionally, even as we constantly fall forward in His army, is amazing. I praise you Jesus and I thank You! Above all this book is dedicated to You, I pray You have Your way Sir. The greatest honor in my life is to be called a child of Yours.

To my wife: I don't even know where to start in thanking you and singing praises of how incredible you are. Without your support right by my side, Soulcon would not be a reality. Other than my salvation and the Holy Spirit, you are the greatest gift the Lord Jesus has given me. I love you babe, and I am eternally grateful for you.

To Ty and Parker: I count it an honor to be your Daddy. I believe in you and I am excited to see how the Lord uses you to share the Good News on this earth! I hope you both grow into the warrior calling on your life with 100% intensity. And no matter what happens in this life, never forget that your Father in Heaven is for you, He loves you with a love richer than anything this world has to offer, and He is always waiting with open arms when you fail. Please, never run from the Lord, but always to Him. I love you both so much and I am proud of you both.

To my Soulcon brothers: I love you guys. I am honored to push my life to the limit in Jesus' name with you! Please do me a favor and remember, every second for the rest of your life, you are at war. Never retreat from the spiritual gunfire, always press in and know you have brothers all around the world serving Christ shoulder-to-shoulder with you in this fight to destroy the work of the Enemy. Keep up the great work for the Lord!! Let's give the Lord 100% intensity every day!

"Be alert and of sober mind. Your enemy the devil prowls around like a roaring lion looking for someone to devour. Resist him, standing firm in the faith, because you know that the family of believers throughout the world is undergoing the same kind of sufferings."

1 Peter 5:8-9 (NIV)

INTRODUCTION

"It is not the critic who counts; not the man who points out how the strong man stumbles, or where the doer of deeds could have done them better. The credit belongs to the man who is actually in the arena, whose face is marred by dust and sweat and blood; who strives valiantly; who errs, who comes short again and again, because there is no effort without error and shortcoming; but who does actually strive to do the deeds; who knows great enthusiasms, the great devotions; who spends himself in a worthy cause; who at the best knows in the end the triumph of high achievement, and who at the worst, if he fails, at least fails while daring greatly, so that his place shall never be with those cold and timid souls who neither know victory nor defeat."

Theodore Roosevelt

Congratulations, I am proud of you! You are taking the next step in your Soulcon lifestyle. I want you to know I am thankful for you, and I am honored to serve Jesus shoulder-to-shoulder with you. I believe what the Lord has in store for us over the next six weeks is going to take your life to a new level of intimacy with the Holy Spirit, and a new level of effectiveness in your ability to love and serve others like Jesus. I am so pumped…

Before we dive in, there are a few things we need to cover. I need to make sure everything is clear, and that you are prepped and ready to take on, what I believe will be the most challenging six weeks to this point in your Christian life. My goal is for this to be the new normal for your warrior life, and trust me it's going to take getting uncomfortable to hit this next level. So let's cover the key items, before we jump into the six-week discipleship experience that will be a continuation of the life of the main character from my first book, Soulcon Challenge. I can hardly wait for you to go with him as he adventures through life and his next visit to the Soulcon Training Center. And this book is going to prep you for the book that will follow this, the Soulcon Marriage. We have one heck of a ride ahead of us so let's get ready to rock…

Hopefully as you're reading this, you are a graduate of the Soulcon

Challenge and a member of the Soulcon Community. If you're not, make sure you stop here, and take on the six-week Soulcon Challenge first. This will prepare your body, soul and spirit to take on what you are about to experience in this book. So hear me, DO NOT READ further if you have not completed the Soulcon Challenge. You can use the Soulcon App (free in any App Store), grab a copy of the Soulcon Challenge, get connected to the Soulcon Community, and grasp the Soulcon culture. After you complete the Soulcon Challenge, this next level experience will be waiting for you.

If you are a Soulcon Graduate, then HOOYAH, let's get ready to roll! Hopefully you have continued to live the Soulcon lifestyle since you graduated. If not, you might want to go back and refresh your memory on the four fundamentals of the Soulcon Challenge. We will be applying the same diet structure throughout this challenge, I believe that is the healthiest way to live, and I want it to be your lifestyle for the remainder of your mission here on earth. This challenge is just going to take those habits and fine tune them over the next six weeks where hopefully they become second nature by the time we are finished, if they are not already. With what we have in store, you will be thankful that your healthy diet is locked in. We have some exciting challenges that are going to require a focused diet to function at the highest level. So do me a favor, right where you are, ask the Lord to prepare your heart to embrace every challenge with 100% intensity, and not one ounce of fear or doubt. As warriors for Christ, we need to operate from faith and focus, not fear and doubt. We will practice this, and engrain that focus into our minds over the next few weeks. Join me and start right now by asking the Lord for His help to walk in His strength, faith, and focus. We need the Lord's strength every second for the rest of our lives, in order to truly walk out the Soulcon lifestyle daily.

OBJECTIVES

"Victorious warriors win first and then go to war, while defeated warriors go to war first and then seek to win."

Sun Tzu

Finishing Objectives

Here are the objectives that need to be accomplished by the end of this challenge to graduate to the next level in your Soulcon journey:

Hold your breath for 90 seconds (not underwater)

The focus of this challenge is to put your brain in a stressful state and use your mind to rise above the fear associated with suffocating. Holding your breath is a great way to develop and practice mental toughness. I encourage you to try to hit this mark during your quiet time in the morning. That's when your resting heart rate is at its lowest, and you can be in a more tranquil state. Just set a timer, take big deep breaths and go for it. You have what it takes, just practice daily, and stay focused. You will knock it out of the park.

**Create a video with your testimony
and then post it on social media.**

When I wrote Soulcon Challenge, I studied the work of the Enemy for about six months. When I found out how easy it was to defeat him, I was shocked. The scripture that brought that brought the most revelation was Revelation 12:11 (NIV), "They triumphed over him by the blood of the Lamb and by the word of their testimony; they did not love their lives so much as to shrink from death." So as we complete this challenge I want to see social media full of men like you sharing their testimony of how Jesus saved them, what He saved them from, and how they walk with Him daily. This could be the best tract you ever share with someone!

Memorize Ephesians 5:1-21

There is nothing better for your brain than extended times in prayer and memorizing God's Word. This is the mark of a true warrior. My goal when I die is to have my brain full of the knowledge of God and

His Word above all else in my life. I want every part of my body to be used up and singing a song of praise to the Lord when it's my time to leave this earth. I know as you're reading this your heart beats for the same thing. So let's put our hearts into action, and drive our brain to memorize these verses.

If you're wondering why I stopped at verse 21, don't worry we will eventually memorize the entire chapter in the next book, Soulcon Marriage. I can't wait. Until then, focus and believe you can. Leave any excuses right here, and finish the mission assigned to you in this challenge. I believe in you!

Weekly Objectives

- Hand out five Gospel Tracts each week (You can purchase those from Soulcon.com)
- Live the Soulcon lifestyle with food, this time with no carbohydrates after 1 p.m. – Eat healthy for six days, and have one feast day
- Run, walk or crawl, at least two 5ks (some weeks the runs are longer)
    o These can also be on an elliptical or bike if your knees won't allow you to run.
- Exercise a total of five days each week for at least 30 minutes each time

Daily Objectives

- Start every day on your knees, praying the Lord's Prayer aloud for your family and your Soulcon brothers.
- Knock out 40 push-ups right after the prayer.
    o Let your Soulcon Dog Tag hit the ground every time. This is a great reminder that falling down is common, but getting back up is what takes the strength. Also, it's a great reminder for your body that it will obey the goals you have and you will not obey the lusts it has.
- Read the daily devotionals
- Drink one gallon of water every day
- No carbohydrates other than from vegetables, berries and sweet potatoes after 1pm (except on your feast day)

WEEKLY OVERVIEW

Week 1   SOULCON TEST IN

Week 2   4 minute cold shower

Week 3   Finish a 10k

Week 4   Finish a timed 7 mile run, walk, or crawl (you can use the elliptical if you need to)

Week 5   Complete a 2 day FAST with your team

Week 6   SOULCON TEST OUT

MISSION BRIEFING
Warrior Elite Preparation

"I have nothing to offer but blood, toil, tears and sweat...You ask, what is our policy? I say it is to wage war by land, sea, and air. War with all our might and with all the strength God has given us, and to wage war against a monstrous tyranny never surpassed in the dark and lamentable catalogue of human crime. That is our policy. You ask, what is our aim? I can answer in one word. It is victory. Victory at all costs - Victory in spite of all terrors - Victory, however long and hard the road may be, for without victory there is no survival."

Winston Churchill

We are about to go back into the fictional experience of the Soulcon Training Center. We are going to walk through challenging times together as we allow our minds to live in a fictional world during our devotional time. It's my heart and prayer that this fictional experience, like the Soulcon Challenge, will make you feel like you are right there with the guys. That you may actually see the sights, smell the smells, and experience the nerves that come with hearing Commander Bugsly's voice instructing you to do some of the most challenging things to this point in your walk with the Lord. I am sure you're excited and ready... But first I have to give you a mission briefing. Then, we can begin.

Now, I want you to use your imagination to put yourself in a mission briefing room in the middle of hostile territory.

"Good morning brothers. I am thankful for each of you. I know on the other side of this briefing we will all dive into one of the greatest challenges we have experienced to this point in our warrior lives. So prepare your mind, your heart and your body. We are going to focus like never before on pushing our lives to the limit with the strength of Christ, to form a will that CANNOT be broken. We live in a world that works on our minds to make us believe that we are not in a war, a world where men are being tricked to believe that if it feels right, then it must be the best thing in the moment. We are all gathered in this briefing room to focus our lives on the antithesis of that fallacy. We are here to focus on the Gospel. To focus on living for Christ, no matter how it feels in the moment. We are here to storm the gates of hell daily, in the name of Jesus.

So don't allow your mind to be conformed to the patterns of this world, brothers. The truth is we are here as soldiers for Jesus Christ, with one focus. We are focused to go out into the hells of this world, and advance the Kingdom by force. Before we leave this briefing room, and walk out into the battlefield, I want to give you a word of caution...

There will never be one second of your life when you are not in war. If you find yourself living in the 'gray' area, where you feel you are neither on the attack for the Kingdom of God or being attacked by the Enemy, you have been tricked. The 'gray' area is where Satan and his soldiers want to get you. Then they will slowly tie you up with an apathetic life, catch you in a small addiction, and slowly destroy your life. There will never be an easy day, so don't long for it. Train your mind and heart to long for the battle of advancing the Gospel... we know there is nothing better. Run toward the spiritual gunfire daily, and never let fear stop you from becoming the warrior the Lord has created you to be.

I love each one of you and I am thankful for you. As we head out into the battle, keep your head on a swivel, don't trust your heart, it can easily lead you to destruction. Our hearts are all wicked. Seek God in everything, listen for His voice, follow His leading, and find your strength in Him alone. Only then, are we indestructible from the work of the Enemy... So put on the armor that the Lord has given you, take up your cross, and let's go forward with 100% intensity daily."

"Hooyah brothers. Leave all your doubts, fears, and insecurities in this briefing room. It's time to run toward the pain, run onto the battlefield, to live every second courageously for His name..."

"You cannot be disciplined in great things and indiscipline in small things. Brave undisciplined men have no chance against the discipline and valor of other men."

General George S. Patton, Jr.

DAY 01

"Therefore be imitators of God as dear children."
Ephesians 5:1 (NKJV)

After a long day, we made it. We both had so many excuses pile up to keep us from being here, but we made it. I look around and see everyone who, like us, made an excuse to get out of their comfort zones. A wave of victory floods my heart and mind... I grab my beautiful wife's hand and we walk back to the child-watch to drop off our kids.

I have learned a lot since the Training Center, and one of the most valuable things I learned was how to play offense in life and never be a victim to an out-of-control schedule. As I reach down to give my kids a kiss and hug, I praise God for the opportunity to raise these warriors. There is a side of me that wants to just go home and relax with them... But I know this time to exercise helps me grow as a special forces soldier for the Lord and be a better husband and dad in the time I have with my family.

As I stand up, I know it's time to rock. I walk toward the treadmill where I am about to knock out one of my 5ks for the week. This is something I have stuck with ever since the Training Center. I still haven't found a better way to train my mind and emotions to not quit than running. It seems like every time I run – I mean every time, I try to talk myself out of it in the first half mile. I think that's why I love it so much. It's helping me forge a will that cannot be broken when the temptation increases.

En route to the treadmills, I kiss my wife before she makes a stop in the restroom and then begins her workout. Man, I love that woman like crazy. I watch her walk away and I praise God for her in my heart. She is such a blessing to my life and has walked through so much with me.

Now, it's time to prepare my mind for battle. I look through my favorite playlist to find music with an incredible beat and a Gospel message. I put my headphones on, and grab a quick drink from the water fountain. As I stand up from my drink, I turn and walk toward the treadmills. My headphones are in, body is focused, and I am ready. Just then, I look over and see a yoga class. A whole room of women in the downward dog, and tight yoga pants... I shut my eyes and turn my head. "Just because you saw that doesn't mean it has to control you," I say to myself. "Lord, I surrender my thoughts to You. I ask for Your help to be like You. Please help me continue to grow in holiness. Thank you for your unconditional love for my life."

I finish my prayer and walk toward the treadmills. I select the one that I will use, and step up. I know if I can complete my 3.1 miles on this I can work on not quitting in any area of my life. For the record, I completely hate these machines... But they get the job done, and on top of that it's freezing outside. So, I hit start, and get my legs moving. Longing for the days when I was with my brothers at Soulcon going for our team runs. Longing for just one more run with my brother, Tyler. I miss that guy like crazy. But until I see him again, I will run. I will push my life to the limit, and then ten times further. I will live a life of honor until I get my new body and arrive at my permanent home with the Lord. Until then... I will stay sober minded and alert. I will live the Soulcon lifestyle every second of every day. The harvest is plentiful. I am one of the few and I am honored. Time to sweat.

"The more you sweat in training, the less you bleed in combat."
Richard Marcinko

Daily Challenge
Let your Soulcon Warrior Elite Group know how you're doing with living as an imitator of God. Are you taking every thought captive like you know you should be? Have you continued the Soulcon life since your last challenge? Let the group know. Do not skip this challenge, or any challenge. Take each one on with 100% intensity.

"The Lord your God is with you, the Mighty Warrior who saves. He will take great delight in you; in his love he will no longer rebuke you, but will rejoice over you with singing."
Zephaniah 3:17 (NIV)

I'm at the point in this run where I feel like I need to slow down. It feels like the heater is blowing down right on my head, and I think the guy next to me hasn't showered in a few days. Not only am I on this treadmill but these external circumstances are making this run suck pretty bad... I have one mile left, and I have a choice to make. Do I allow these circumstances to stop me, or do I press on? I know what I need to do but it seems this choice is never easy. I make the decision to embrace the suck, and press on. I reach down and turn the speed up just to show my body that not only is quitting not an option, but I am going to make my body finish faster than it started. It's a way to buffet my body like a boxer, and a way to get off this machine quicker.

As I see 3.1 miles come up on the treadmill, I hit the stop button. I'm winded, and sweating like crazy. I grab my towel to wipe down the treadmill and I walk over to get a drink, this time making sure I don't look toward the yoga class. Not going to take even one little bite from the fork that feeds my flesh. Not one thought, not one glance, nothing. There is no reason for me to look, even though there is a side of me that wants to justify just one look. But I've learned what that one look can turn into. And after confessing my occasional pornography viewing to the guys at the Training Center, I know that is something I never want to return to. So, I will live guarded, every day.

After I grab a drink of water, I open up the Soulcon App to share my run times with my community. This is something we do to keep each other accountable with doing our weekly runs, but also not getting comfortable and slowing down in our weekly runs. We hold each other accountable to push ourselves every time we exercise. I am so thankful for the Soulcon Community and the warrior brotherhood that we all get to live in together. I feel like these guys are right here with me. Again, that thought makes my heart long for Tyler. I wish he could see what Soulcon has grown into. He would love to see this brotherhood expanding around the world… and I hear my beautiful bride calling for me. Time to go grab the kiddos and head home.

As we pull into the driveway, we grab the mail and head inside to eat dinner. My brain starts to think how good a bowl of cereal would be right now, or just a little bowl of ice cream after dinner. But I have to stay focused. I have found that my wife will follow my leadership. If I cave, it will entice her to cave with her eating. And we know that eating healthy isn't to look pretty, but to practice habits of holiness in our lives. To make habits of honoring God with everything that we do and to make sure we never justify making habits of sin. That's why we are so focused with our eating, and I am thankful for it. But man, some sugary carbs sound great right now.

As we get inside, I have my hands full and the mail falls to the ground. When it does, I see a letter from Soulcon on the floor. This letter looks different than the regular communications Soulcon sends out. My mind starts to race thinking about what it could be. I reach down and grab the letter, and see that it's handwritten. I set my stuff down, leave the other mail all over the floor, and dive into the letter from Soulcon…

Daily Challenge
I believe God longs to show us areas which He is proud of us, but most of the time we don't take the time to listen to Him in this way, because we are constantly hard on ourselves. I want you to take 10 minutes today and go to a quiet place and ask the Lord to show you areas where He is proud of you. I believe He is waiting to tell you.

DAY 03

"And walk in love, as Christ also has loved us and given Himself for us, an offering and a sacrifice to God for a sweet-smelling aroma."

Ephesians 5:2 (NKJV)

As I dive into the letter from Soulcon, I'm anxious to see what's inside this letter that was addressed in a person's handwriting that my mind knows very well. My mind remembers seeing this handwriting on a white board so many times over the course of my six-week stay at the Soulcon Training Center. It looks like Commander Bugsly himself addressed it. I am so pumped. I open the envelope quickly making sure I don't tear the letter inside, and I hear my son start screaming. I drop the letter and sprint to the back of the house where he is laying on the ground crying out for daddy as he screams in pain. As I get to him I check him for any broken bones or bleeding and thankfully there is neither. Realizing he is okay, I pick him up off the freezing ground and hold him. My heart is breaking for his pain, but I am so thankful he is not hurt too badly.

"What happened little buddy?" I ask him in a calm voice to try to get him to calm down as well.

"Daddy, I am sorry. I did something I wasn't supposed to do. I jumped off the trampoline like you told me not to. Sorry daddy… I'm so sorry." "It's okay buddy. I want you to know no matter what, daddy loves you and I forgive you. Do me a favor, learn to trust what daddy says is good for you… Deal?"

"Deal daddy," My little man says as he reaches out his fist for a fist bump.

"Now quick get in the house, it's freezing out here," I say as I set him back down, and he climbs back up on the trampoline. I watch him, and smile. I turn back to go into the house to read the letter, and I feel the Lord work in my heart as I walk. I pause to listen to the Lord. I have learned through Soulcon that my devotion time with the Lord is not an isolated event in the morning, but an every second of my life event. I want to be continually sober minded and alert, always ready to hear from the Lord. As I stop walking, and quiet my heart to hear if it's the Lord trying to speak to my heart, I hear.

"My love for you is infinitely greater than your love for your son. No matter how many times you fail, I love you relentlessly through it all." Hearing this from the Lord, I grab one of our chairs on our back porch and sit down. I feel overwhelmed with God's presence. Wow....

"Lord, thank you," I whisper. "Help me view my life from your love, and not from my actions, no matter how good or bad they are. Thank you Lord Jesus. Thank you for your love."

Moments like these change everything in my life. Hearing from the King of kings and Lord of lords that He loves me, even though He sees my worst actions, makes my soul radiate with worship to His name. I can't help but live as a sacrifice of praise when I know and believe how much God loves me. I pray I can keep focused on His love as the driving force of my life for my entire mission on this earth. What an amazing God we serve…

Now, time to head back inside to see what this letter from Soulcon says…

Daily Challenge
As you work through memorizing Ephesians 5:1-21, I want you to take time and meditate on Ephesians 5:2 today. Our goal as special forces soldiers of Jesus is to walk in God's love daily. Ask the Lord to show you how to love others with a deeper love and that He softens your heart to everyone in your life. We need soldiers like you and me showing this world how much God loves them by our words, actions and legacy we will leave.

"Therefore, since we are surrounded by such a great cloud of witnesses, let us throw off everything that hinders and the sin that so easily entangles. And let us run with perseverance the race marked out for us, 2 fixing our eyes on Jesus, the pioneer and perfecter of faith. For the joy set before him he endured the cross, scorning its shame, and sat down at the right hand of the throne of God."

Hebrews 12:1-2 (NIV)

Walking back in the house, I step through the mail spread out on the floor where I dropped it, and I look for the letter I dropped when I sprinted outside. I spot it, and eagerly bend down and pick it up. I open it up and start to read:

My brother,

I hope this letter finds you well. It feels like just yesterday that you and I jumped out of the plane together. What a great time! I hope you're continuing in that level of courage in your daily walk with the Lord that you showed that day, and throughout your time at the Training Center. You were one of our top students that we've had. Tyler was too. You guys did incredible together and truly impacted your team. We were all so proud of you both. And again, I am so sorry about Tyler. That broke all of our hearts. But at least he died doing what he did best, laying his life down for others in service. I pray we all have a death song as honorable as he had... What a good man.

I am writing today to let you know that you have been selected to go through the toughest program we have to offer at Soulcon. The program is Soulcon Warrior Elite. This is a two-week training that will take you to a higher level of intimacy with Christ. There are only 12 warriors that have been selected for this course, and Soulcon is going to pay for you to come to the Training Center for the program. The only thing we ask in return is for you to become the Soulcon representative in your area from this point forward, if you graduate. And please hear me, there is an "if" with this course – not everyone will graduate. This program has no easy day. It will push you further than you've been pushed to this point. And on top of that, it's a cold weather challenge.

Please pray about this with your wife, and let us know ASAP. The program starts in two weeks. We will need to book your flight soon and lock in your spot.

No matter your decision, I am honored to serve Christ with you brother. Keep living the Soulcon lifestyle!

Hooyah,
Commander Bugsly

As I finish reading, I feel like I just drank an energy drink. My adrenaline is firing on all cylinders. What an honor! And what in the world could this program have to offer? If Bugsly says it will push me further than I've been pushed before…yikes! I wonder if I could finish. I wonder if I have what it takes. I wonder if my wife will be on board for me going back again. I have so many thoughts racing through my mind. In the middle of my excitement it hits me…

The weight of Tyler's loss is something I don't think I will ever be completely healed from. I miss that guy like crazy. It would have been so incredible to call him and share in this excitement with him. Just to hear his always optimistic voice would do my soul such good... I commit from this day forward to push my life to the limit for Jesus and bring honor to the Lord and all the saints (like Tyler) who are now in His presence, cheering the saints on earth to finish strong.

"Hey babe!" I yell to my wife, "You're not going to believe this letter I just got from Bugsly…"

Daily Challenge
Set aside 5 minutes today to meditate on the saints in Heaven who are cheering you on. Use your imagination to see them. Think of specific people in the Bible and use your mind to converse with them. Think of the family members you have that are with the Lord, they are cheering you on as well. Use your imagination to see them and speak with them. Not only do we get to spend eternity with Jesus, we get to spend eternity with the heroes of the Bible, and all the saints

who accept Jesus as their Lord and Savior. So pause today, and meditate on that. It should shoot adrenaline into your souls as you push through this challenge.

"But fornication and all uncleanness or covetousness, let it not even be named among you, as is fitting for saints; neither filthiness, nor foolish talking, nor coarse jesting, which are not fitting, but rather giving of thanks. For this you know, that no fornicator, unclean person, nor covetous man, who is an idolater, has any inheritance in the kingdom of Christ and God. Let no one deceive you with empty words, for because of these things the wrath of God comes upon the sons of disobedience. Therefore do not be partakers with them."

Ephesian 5:3-7 (NKJV)

It's hard to believe that I am waiting to board a plane to go back to the Training Center. I cannot thank God enough for a wife who supports my journey to be the warrior Christ has called me to be. She is such a rock in our relationship, and I will always be grateful for her. It would be really cool to go through a challenge like this with her, or even if Soulcon had a challenge for just women. She would love that. She is a true warrior, and I would love to see how the Lord would use that in her life. But man, doing life without my wife would not be easy. Talk about a season of getting out of my comfort-zone…

That thought makes my emotions calm down a bit as I think that no matter what I'm about to face over the next two weeks is going to be easier than running the home without my bride there. Bring on the cold weather Soulcon Warrior Elite training…

I hear the gate agent let me know it's now my time to board. I grab my bags and head to board the plane. I hand the agent my boarding pass, and walk down to board. I stand with all of the people waiting to find their seat and start walking slowly with them until I get to my seat. I am always interested who the Lord will allow to sit next to me during the flight, so I look ahead as the line slowly moves to get to my seat. Then, my heart sinks as I see who I will be sitting next to for this flight. One of the most beautiful women I have seen is going to be sitting right next to me. Crap. I reach into my carry on and frantically grab my headphones. I work to put them in my ears and of course, they are tangled. I pray the line could move slower, but it's not. It's now time for me to sit down and my headphones are not in. Bummer.

"Excuse me ma'am, I am in the window seat next to you," I say as my voice trembles, afraid of even speaking to this woman.

"No problem," she said, as she stood up to let me in.

As she stood, I couldn't help but notice her bright colored yoga pants look like they are painted on. Then a wave crashes into my nostrils of the beautiful woman's fragrance. Oh no... I feel like Bruce Banner trying to keep the Hulk at bay. I instantly go back to everything Bugsly taught us about controlling our brain. Now I'm no longer sober minded and in a state of emergency internally. I need to get worship music in my ears, but my headphones are now in a knot. I scoot in, place my bag down, and sit in my window seat. I feel like I am trapped as she sits down right next to me on this small plane.

"Maybe she won't talk to me," I say in my mind as I work on this knot. But even as I said that, I felt my brain starting to lust for just one bite of the fork that feeds my flesh.

"Just talk to her," I hear whisper in my mind. I know that thought is not from me. I have learned the secret attack of the Enemy, and I will not surrender my will to those thoughts and lusts of my flesh for one second.

"Excuse me, I just want to tell you that I love your shirt. What branch of the military were you in?" she says to me with a soft, beautiful voice. As she spoke those words I felt like I just got hit with an arrow of Kryptonite in my heart. It feels like my tongue is swelling up in my mouth. I don't know what to say.

"Thank you ma'am. It's actually not a military logo, but a logo for a special forces group in the Body of Christ called Soulcon. I am actually headed back to their training center on this flight." I say as I am praying in my heart that causes her to stop talking to me.

"Well you look like a military man. Your wife is one lucky woman... I wish my husband would take care of his body like you do," she says back with a flirtatious voice, that makes my entire body feel weak, as her gaze seems to penetrate my soul.

"Don't engage. Don't continue talking. Remember not a hint of impurity in your heart," I say to myself. Then I smile and nod, and bluntly look the other direction. I get my headphones out of the knot they're in, and put them on.

With worship music on and my mind focusing on purity, in Christ, I can do this. There is a war for purity in my heart, and I will not back down from the fight. I will engage. I will win this war. I am committed…

I sit back, shut my eyes, and feel the presence of the Lord cover me. He is right there in the middle of my temptation. The Lord didn't take the beautiful woman away from me, He didn't stop the smell of her incredible perfume, but He helped me focus on His presence more than my current temptation to have lustful thoughts. God is so faithful.

Daily Challenge
How are you doing with the war for the purity of your thought life? Are you committed to living with not a hint of impurity in your heart? Communicate these answers with your team today and share with your Soulcon brothers in the Soulcon Community.

DAY 06

"I discipline my body like an athlete, training it to do what it should. Otherwise, I fear that after preaching to others I myself might be disqualified."

1 Corinthians 9:27 (NLT)

Just over the sound of my worship music, I hear the flight attendant's voice letting us know we are on our descent, and that we need to put our tray tables up and place our chairs in the upright position. My heart gets excited as I start to think about the incredible challenge and adventure ahead of me. I am now only a one-hour van ride away from the Soulcon Training Center. Hooyah...

I slowly lean forward to put my chair in the upright position, and commit to not take out the worship music in my ear until this incredibly beautiful woman is no longer sitting next to me. I know some of the best ways to stay guarded from flirtatious conversations that wouldn't honor the Lord or my wife, is to just avoid them. I turn my head to look out the window as our plane is on its descent. Last time I was in this position there was no snow on the ground, and I had my best friend next to me. Those were two things that made that first challenge and adventure much easier... I bet Tyler is looking down at me right now, eating a donut, smiling. And I know there is a side of him that wishes he was here with me. Man, I miss that guy. I lean my head back and tears come to my eyes.

"God," I whisper under my breath, "I know You are good, and I trust You. But losing Tyler was so hard, and it didn't make sense. I trust you. I'm just missing my best friend. I ask that you give me the strength to live a life that honors You, and all the saints who have gone before me. Lord, please never let me lose my focus. Help me never forget that You're always with me, and that the heavenly realm, Tyler included, is cheering me on. Thank you, Sir."

I reach my arm up to wipe the tears from my eyes just as our plane touches down. The timing of the plane landing, my prayer ending, my eyes opening and my arms wiping the tears away was almost cinematic with the timing. Now, I feel like Rocky Balboa flying into

Russia to go train my body for battle. But my enemy is not a blonde Russian; my Enemy is the most lethal enemy in the history of the world. I need to discipline my body like a boxer daily, and I will.

Our plane comes to a stop at the gate, the seatbelt light comes off, and we can stand up to grab our bags in the overhead.

"Just one look won't hurt." I hear in my mind as a thought of her yoga pants floods my brain. "It won't hurt anything, you have to look that way anyway to get out. Just look in that direction, you're okay. You've done great this whole flight, just one look to see what her butt looks like in those yoga pants won't hurt anyone."

For our struggle is not against flesh and blood, but against the rulers, against the authorities, against the powers of this dark world and against the spiritual forces of evil in the heavenly realms.

Ephesians 6:12 (NIV)

I quickly identify the voice of the Enemy, trying to get me to take one bite of the fork that feeds my flesh, and that prick uses my own voice to speak to get me to self-destruct. I will not surrender my will to his temptation, to his darkness, not even for one second. I fix my eyes on the seat in front of me, and I make my body stay in the seat. I grab my phone to make it look like I am doing work. I wait for everyone to get off the plane, and then I look to my left and stand up, victorious.

That's how winning is done… Bring it on Soulcon Training Center! Hooyah!!

Daily Challenge

Set the timer on your phone, and spend three minutes talking to God about your emotions right where you are now. Maybe you're tired, maybe you're hurting, and maybe you're covered in guilt from a recent failure. Just take time and be brutally honest with God, and after the timer goes off, tell God aloud, how thankful you are for Him. How thankful you are that you can come boldly into His throne of grace, by the blood of Jesus and talk to the King of kings and Lord of lords…who is your Father.

DAY 07

"For you were once darkness, but now you are light in the Lord. Walk as children of light (for the fruit of the Spirit is in all goodness, righteousness, and truth), finding out what is acceptable to the Lord."

Ephesians 5:8-10 (NKJV)

Walking off the plane, I feel like I am walking in the light like Jesus. I feel like I just won a war, and before Soulcon, I would have taken that bite from the fork the enemy was trying to entice me with. And I know how those thoughts grow and what they turn into. I am so thankful for the understanding of Soulcon. There is not one second for the rest of my life where I am not in war. I have to keep my mind alert and ready to rock. I am on this earth for a short time, and my mission is to fully accomplish the Lord's plan for my life. My goal is to finish strong by taking on every challenge with 100% intensity in the strength of Christ.

Be sober [well balanced and self-disciplined], be alert and cautious at all times. That enemy of yours, the devil, prowls around like a roaring lion [fiercely hungry], seeking someone to devour.

1 Peter 5:8 (AMP)

I can't wait for what the Lord has in store for me over these next two weeks. It's going to be so good to see Commander and the Founder again. Man, I miss those guys and I am so grateful for the way they constantly invest in the lives of the men of Soulcon.

Now I just have to make it to baggage claim and into the Soulcon van without stepping out of the light of Christ with my mind, will, and emotions. And not to mention, make it without buying one of these pastries that smell incredible and seem to be all over this airport.

"Just don't make eye contact," I say to myself as I laugh. Whether a pastry or a hot woman, I don't want to practice surrendering my will to anything in this world. Just then, someone hits me on my back...

"My brother! I didn't know you were going to be here!"

"Alfred?" I asked the man that just slapped my back like someone who didn't know his own strength.

"Yes sir!" Alfred says, with a huge smile beaming from a face that looks like a chiseled warrior.

"Bro! I hardly recognized you! You look incredible! You truly look like a special forces soldier!"

"Thanks a ton brother, this Soulcon stuff has changed my life completely. And better than that, it's changed my family's lives as well! My son is running my 5ks with me, and my wife keeps praying that Soulcon eventually includes something for women. She has been struggling with her health for a while now and I am at a loss. I just keep praying for her and encouraging her."

"First off, I'm so proud of you bro!" I say as I give him a big hug. As I hug him, my mind goes back to the run when I judged him for being the slow fat guy on our run. Now look at this guy, a lean body warrior for Christ... Praise God! "Secondly, I hear you bro. Leading in the area of our wives is a big challenge. That would be awesome if women could be a part of Soulcon in some way in the future. I know my wife needs it for sure, too."

"Amen. Let's grab our bags and head out to the van. Hey bro, surely Tyler got selected right? Where is he?" Alfred says, as my soul sinks with grief.

"Long story. I'll share it in the van on the ride over to the Training Center," I say back with a heavy heart and eyes slowly welling up with tears…

Daily Challenge

Check with your team to see how everyone is doing with memorizing their verses. Do your best to have through verse 10 done. You can do it. Never forget, one of the best things we can do for our brains as soldiers for Jesus Christ is to train our brains to memorize Scripture. Make an excuse to get there today. Through verse 10 is the goal, crush it brothers! Hooyah.

WEEK 01 RESULTS AND REFLECTIONS

Be sure to share your results and encourage others
going through the challenge on the SOULCON App.

Weekly Objectives

- Hand out five Gospel Tracts each week (You can purchase those from Soulcon.com)
- Live the Soulcon lifestyle with food, this time with no carbohydrates after 1 p.m. – Eat healthy for six days, and have one feast day
- Run, walk or crawl, at least two 5ks (some weeks the runs are longer)
    - o These can also be on an elliptical or bike if your knees won't allow you to run.
- Exercise a total of five days each week for at least 30 minutes each time

Daily Objectives

- Start every day on your knees, praying the Lord's Prayer aloud for your family and your Soulcon brothers.
- Knock out 40 push-ups right after the prayer.
    - o Let your Soulcon Dog Tag hit the ground every time. This is a great reminder that falling down is common, but getting back up is what takes the strength. Also, it's a great reminder for your body that it will obey the goals you have and you will not obey the lusts it has.
- Read the daily devotionals
- Drink one gallon of water every day
- No carbohydrates other than from vegetables, berries and sweet potatoes after 1pm (except on your feast day)

DAY 08

"Greater love has no one than this: to lay down one's life for one's friends."

John 15:13 NIV

As the van door shuts, my heart sinks. I know what I have to do, but I don't want to do it. Sharing about the loss of one of my best friends, no matter how many times I do it, never gets easier. So I say a quick prayer, take a deep breath and look into Alfred's eyes to share about the death song of Tyler.

"Man, this never gets easier," I say as tears already start to well up in my eyes.

"Take your time brother," Alfred says back to me with a calming tone of voice.

"Man, I just… I mean, I never… I wasn't ready to lose Tyler. I thought we would grow old together, sharing the Gospel even in the assisted living house together toward the end of our lives. I miss that guy like crazy… I will never forget the feeling I had the morning I woke up when I found out about Tyler's death. It was like most mornings in the Soulcon life. I woke up early to have my devotion time with the Lord, I prayed the Lord's prayer out loud on my knees, knocked out my 40 push-ups and focused my mind and heart to experience the Lord's presence. But that morning just felt off. I was struggling to focus my mind. So, I opened up my phone, and took it off airplane mode. Once I did, messages starting coming through at an unusually high rate. My mind raced and my heart rate elevated as I started to worry about what all of the messages were about. I was thinking through if I made a mistake on the project for work I just finished the day before. I hurried and opened the first message, and it read:

I'm so sorry to hear about Tyler…

My heart sank. Without any other message open I felt the reality in my heart. Tyler was gone. As I opened the next message it was a link to an article:

Two Good Samaritans killed after stopping to help a motorist

Instantly tears flooded my eyes. My brother, my best friend, was gone. I dropped to my knees and cried out to the Lord asking why….

Then after a few minutes I got back up and read the article to find out that Tyler was on his way home on Friday night with his family, when they saw a motorist on the side of the road who lost control and flipped her car. Tyler, acting like the man of courage he was, pulled over to take action. Pulled over with his family, and committed to serve other people with the warrior body and life he had. He got out of the car, and went up with another person that had pulled over, and they rescued the passenger in the car. As they were walking back to Tyler's car, the unexpected happened. Another car lost control and flipped over, rolling right into Tyler and the guy with him who helped rescue the passenger, killing them both instantly…"

"Wow. I am so sorry to hear that," Alfred said as he started to cry.

I put my arm around him and joined him. We both wept as we remembered our fallen brother, Tyler. A true special forces soldier for the Lord.

"After I read that, I got my clothes on and drove over to his house. I just wanted to hug everyone in his family. I loved them all, and still do, like crazy. When I got to their house, I knocked on the door, not having any words to say, just actions to give. His precious daughter opened the door, and she hugged me, and we both wept. Then I spent the day with their family. My heart hurting uncontrollably. My only option was to trust in God's sovereignty."

Daily Challenge
Ask the Lord to search your heart today. As special forces soldiers for Jesus Christ, some of us carry hurt that we were never intended to carry on our own. Ask the Lord if there is anywhere in your life where you haven't trusted him with the pain in your heart. Maybe from the loss of a loved one, a marriage ended without explanation, or any other painful event that you never fully surrendered to the Lord. I pray today that surrender happens. I pray you hand over that pain to the Lord. He can be trusted with all of our pain, not just some of it.

"Since, then, you have been raised with Christ, set your hearts on things above, where Christ is, seated at the right hand of God. Set your minds on things above, not on earthly things."
Colossians 3:1-2 NIV

As tears were still sliding down my face, I noticed that Alfred wasn't taking the news well at all. He was still sobbing.

"I know how you feel brother, I was in the same place. I was there, and the hurt was almost more than I could bear," I said to Alfred.

"That's not it brother. After the Training Center, Tyler reached out to me. He said I had made a big impact on his life and he wanted to pay my way to take me hunting to get to know me more. I knew in my heart when he asked I should have said yes, but I allowed the excuse of being too busy to determine my answer. I let him know that I was too busy and thanked him for the invitation, and went on with life. I had no idea that would be the last time I would talk to him. UGH!! What I would give to turn back time and take him up on that trip…"

"Sorry brother," I said to him as I put my arm around him. "But just to encourage you, Tyler's funeral was the biggest celebration of a life I have ever been a part of. A church that holds around 2,000 people had to use their overflow seating. Everyone there celebrated a warrior's life for King Jesus. At his funeral there were around 15-20 people who surrendered their life to Jesus as Lord and Savior, and I know everyone there was inspired to live their lives to the fullest for the King of kings every day. I just pray my death song will be as worshipful as Tyler's."

"Praise God… I will just have to keep my eyes fixed on honoring Jesus every second as well as all the fallen saints cheering us on. It's pretty cool to think that Tyler is with King David, Noah, Elijah, Paul, Peter, and King Jesus cheering us on. I loved that guy… But man, I wish I wouldn't have let my excuse of a busy life stop me from making time to build my relationship with him. Now, I will have to wait until heaven. I will soldier on, but that hurts…"

"I hear ya brother… I know Tyler would have loved that time with you. I knew Tyler better than most people on this earth. Let me promise you one thing I'm sure of he would be pissed if you were living in regret. I know he has a bag of popcorn in heaven, waiting to watch us take violent action against the work of the Enemy. Let's do just that. Every day. Let's live to give heaven a show as we stomp the piss out of the demonic realm."

"Hooyah brother, hooyah," Alfred says back as we fist bump.

"Alright guys, we're here," the driver says as we come to a stop.

As I look out the window, my heart starts to pound. We're back…

"Therefore, since we are surrounded by such a huge crowd of witnesses to the life of faith, let us strip off every weight that slows us down, especially the sin that so easily trips us up. And let us run with endurance the race God has set before us."
Hebrews 12:1 NLT

Daily Challenge
Text, email or write a letter to one of your loved ones today. Let them know how much you love them and how grateful you are for them. Don't take one day for granted with them. We never know when their mission will be completed and they will go be with the Lord Jesus. AND… Stomp the piss out of the demonic realm today! Shout about the victory of King Jesus on the rooftops with every action and word today. Hooyah brothers. Love ya!

DAY 10

"And have no fellowship with the unfruitful works of darkness, but rather expose them. For it is shameful even to speak of those things which are done by them in secret."
Ephesians 5:11-12 (NKJV)

As I reach over to open the door of the van, I take a deep breath and exhale out my anxiety. Then I slide the door open. A rush of freezing wind comes into the van causing a new level of anxiety in my brain for this two-week adventure I'm about to embark on.

"It's okay brother, we've got this," Alfred said to me as he slapped my shoulder.

I look at him and pat him back on his shoulder, "Thanks bro."

We step out of the van and start walking to the Headquarters (HQ) to get checked in.

"Man, I've missed this place. We made some great memories here."

"It's time to make some new ones," Alfred says back.

"Amen," I say back as my heart is heavy thinking about Tyler.

Just then, we notice a new addition to the Soulcon Training Center. It looks like a big brick mailbox combined with a fire pit. We both walk up to it to satisfy the curiosity in our minds, and see words inscribed on the metal plaque:

LEAVE YOUR SIN IN THE FIRE

Before taking one more step, write out your sin on one of these pieces of paper. Then place it into the furnace. We will burn it tonight. It's time to be walking fully in the light of Christ and learn to hate sin.

"I'm in," I say as we both reach for a pen and one of the pieces of paper.

I try to slow my mind down to focus and ask the Lord what sin He wants to burn out of my life. Lust and pride comes to my mind, so I write them down, and put my paper into the entrance of the furnace. I wonder what Commander Bugsly has in store for us with this one...

"What did you write down?" I asked Alfred as we started walking again to get checked in.

"Resentment. It's something I still wrestle with about my sweet girl. Resentment toward myself, for being such a pathetic leader after she defeated cancer with a smile and went to be with the Lord. It's an area that I'm working on with the Lord, but I need to put it to death. What about you bro?"

"Lust and pride. I have had such victory with lust since coming through Soulcon, but it still lingers. A lust to do things with my wife that I remember from some of the porn videos I've seen. I need to learn to hate that sin. And then pride. It's a sin that I can feed just one bite here, just one bite there when people see the leader that I have become in my community since going through this training. I need to learn to hate pride..."

"Amen brother," Alfred says as we step in the HQ to check-in.

"Man, praise God for heat!" I say to the guy behind the desk to check in.

"Don't get used to it man..." the guy behind the desk says without smirking.

"What do you mean?"

"You guys are here for Warrior Elite. This is the most difficult training Bugsly has to dish out. About 50% of the guys wash out before the two weeks is over."

"Thanks for the pep talk brother," I say back, honestly a little pissed.

"I just want to shoot you guys straight. It's going to be cold and physically demanding, but that won't be the hardest part. The hardest part is the spiritual challenge. You are going to face some areas of your life that honestly you don't want to face head on. You can either quit and retreat, or man up and take those issues to the cross. But here are your check-in packets. The first team meeting is tonight at 2030. Dress warm and Godspeed."

"Thanks bro," I say as I grab my packet and open it up to see what room I'm in.

"Check this out Alfred, we're all in the same room. Must be a typo."

"No, it's not. This time, you and your team all sleep in the same barracks room. There's nothing comfortable about this next two weeks. Kick butt guys!" The check-in guy says cracking his first smile since we walked in.

What in the world did I sign up for...

Daily Challenge
Grab a pen and paper. Write down a sin in your life that needs to be put to death. One that you have been tolerating and not hating that needs to be put to death. Be honest with yourself. After you finish, share that word with your team. Then take that piece of paper and hold on to it until tomorrow.

"But all things that are exposed are made manifest by the light, for whatever makes manifest is light."
Ephesians 5:13 (NKJV)

After getting our stuff settled in our barracks room, I was surprised to find out that I didn't know anyone other than Alfred. We all start getting ready to head out for our 2030 meeting. Honestly, I am not sure what to think about sleeping in the same room as eleven other men who will be finishing the days sweaty and worn out like me. I am also feeling my heart missing my family, and the weight of two weeks away from them starts to sink in.

"When I am weak He is strong," I say under my breath to remind my soul to stay focused. Ever since Soulcon I have used self-talk daily to help keep my mind, will, and emotions focused on the Lord.

I reach over, grab my jacket, and join our team to walk out to our first team meeting. We step outside and the freezing wind pierces through my jeans. I smile in the face of that little pain knowing we are about to see Commander Bugsly again. I love that guy.

As we walk up to the new addition to the Training Center, the brick furnace where Alfred and I stopped when we got here, I see two men talking. It's Commander and the Founder! I'm pumped!

Our class takes our seats, and the two of them finish talking and turn to all of us.

"Welcome back gentlemen! It's been too long!" Commander Bugsly yells out to us. "I want to congratulate each of you for making the decision to return to the Training Center for the Warrior Elite training! The Founder and I are thrilled you take your relationship with the Lord serious enough that you would be willing to push your body, soul and spirit to the next level as Soulcon soldiers. Trust me gentlemen, what we are about to embark on is going to push you to the next level in your relationship with the Lord. I want you to look around... these are faces of brothers in Christ who are only going to make it through if you decide to work together. We have yet to have one class complete with 100% of their members that started. The Founder and I have been praying that your class would be the one to make this happen… We'll see.

"I am sure you've had a chance to look through your check-in packets. There are meeting times listed, and clothing we encourage you to wear for each training evolution. We have intentionally left out the details of the training evolutions. We don't want you to quit before we begin.

"Like I said, this is going to push you. But you have been selected because we all believe in you, and we have structured this class with the top students that have been through the Training Center, which is why we are hopeful that you guys will have a 100% completion rate. Let's see what you've got.

"Our first order of business is the most important, to forge an iron will in Christ. We have to get everything into the Light of Christ. Our goal over the next two weeks is to have you fully focused on who you are in Christ, and as warrior of Christ one who doesn't focus your mind on the darkness of sin. We had each of you write down a sin or sins that you need to leave in the fire, and they are sitting in this furnace. I want you to meditate on what the sin was that you wrote on that paper, and meditate on the death of this sin. I want you to see the sin eternally separated from your life. Never a part of your identity again. Gentlemen, there is not one sin that can be a part of your identity as a warrior of Christ. Not one. We have to remove all sin from our meditative thoughts on who we are as warriors for Christ. And there is only one way to do that. Confess, repent and be filled constantly by the Holy Spirit. If we confess our sin to our brother there is healing, and we take a 180 degree turn from that sin never to go back, then we fill that hole where sin was with the presence of the Lord. This is a process that takes the Holy Spirit, and that's what we're going to practice tonight.

"So here's what we're going to do. We are going to light the furnace on fire and meditate on how our sin on that paper is consumed with the fire in the furnace. Then I want each of you to meditate on your sin in God's presence in your heart. How if we are truly full of the Lord, there will be an all-consuming fire that will melt all the sin away from our heart.

"Brothers, it's time to become the elite warriors the Lord has called us to be. We are going to take the next hour, sitting here in the cold, and meditate on your sin being consumed by this fire. Ask the Lord to move in your heart. Before we go on, we need to leave your sin in the dark, and never turn back to it. The Founder and I will be back in one hour. This is your first, and in my opinion, most important test. Kick butt!"

Daily Challenge

Take your paper from yesterday with your sin written on it and set it in front of you. Meditate on God's presence coming in your room and consuming that sin with His presence like a fire. Completely destroying it, and taking away every bit of power it has on your life. Allow your heart to experience the freedom in the Lord from being truly full of His light.

After you're finished shred up the paper and throw it in the trash... Never to go back to it.

(For safety precautions, do not set the paper on fire.)

DAY 12

"So if the Son sets you free, you are truly free."

John 8:36 (NLT)

"Alright men," Commander says as he and the Founder walk back up with coffee in both of their hands. "You made it. You completed the first challenge of your stay here at Soulcon Warrior Elite training. Well done! I want everyone to take a quick break, and head over to grab a cup of coffee from the HQ. Then come back out to hear about our next challenge."

Wait a second? Coffee? What about hitting the rack and catching some much needed sleep? Oh well, at least it will warm this body up, it's freezing out here.

"Hey bro, wait up!" Alfred shouts out to me.

"Man, what do you think Bugsly and the Founder have up their sleeves?"

"I'm not sure, but it's going to take some caffeine, so let's fuel up!"

"Amen brother. I'm in," I say back as we walk into HQ.

As we're grabbing our coffee I start to think about the hour we just experienced. I don't even know if I truly comprehend it. What would my life look like if sin was truly melted away? Is that even possible? I mean I know the Lord has saved me, and that I am serving as a special forces soldier in His army, but could I truly be perfect as He is perfect? Man… That's heavy. If I can, I want to learn.

Alfred walks over and holds his black cup of coffee for a cheers, I reach out my cup and meet him in the middle for a cheers.

"Here's to leaving it all on the field, and every sin in the dark!" I say as we cheer.

"Hooyah brother," Alfred says back as we both take a sip.

46

"Let's get back out there and see what our next challenge is." I say as we head back out into the bone-chilling breeze creeping through the Training Center.

"Welcome back guys!" Bugsly yells out with his typical smirk that makes him look like he enjoys our pain a little too much.

"Please take a seat, we need to cover a few things from the last challenge before we jump into our next challenge. Gentlemen, one of the things we have seen with Soulcon soldiers as they have graduated and returned back to their homes, is that some of them have fallen back into the sin the Lord delivered them from. With everyone on staff here at Soulcon, it never stops hurting our hearts to see this. So the Founder and I have been seeking the Lord to see what we can modify in the training to forge an iron will in Christ in every man. We have come to the conclusion that men need to fully know they are completely set free from their sinful nature. We have seen too many men thinking the main battle is with their sinful nature. And we all know the more you focus on something the more you drift toward the thing you are thinking about. Therefore, we have enhanced our training philosophy. From this point forward, we want each of you to identify with your new man in Christ and never again your sinful man. Never again.

"So no matter what the sin was on that paper, it's gone. That is no longer a part of your life. The Founder and I want you to grow into being full imitators of Christ. You have no time as a warrior for Christ to meditate on a habit you used to have when you walked in the darkness. We believe at Soulcon this will be the game changer for each of you.

"Just to clarify, from this point forward you are to only meditate on who you are in Christ. Commit right now to never be enslaved by who you were again. Sin and death have no control over your soul, so do not surrender control ever again.

"This will become a reality over the next two weeks within your soul, just do me a favor and do not quit. What you're about to experience will change the way you think as a man of God for the rest of your life.

We all need you to finish strong, brothers.

"Stand up and you will see just behind me are twelve bags. I want you each to grab one and get ready to go for our first team run."

Wait a second, team run? It's almost midnight, and it's unbelievably cold. I can't believe I missed this guy during my time away from this Training Center. I now know Bugsly is truly crazy…

I tip my cup up, finish my last sip of coffee and stand up to go grab my bag. As I walk with the team I suddenly realize that these bags look extremely familiar. Crap… They're parachute bags.

Daily Challenge

Today is the first cold shower challenge. Brutal, I know. This first one is only two minutes. I want you to get in the shower, and take the first two minutes with the ice-cold water hitting you in the chest. Set a timer for two minutes and embrace the good pain. Meditate during this time on who you are in Christ. Commit to never again surrender your will to the sin you used to be defined by. You are new, and you will never again be defined by that sin…as long as you don't surrender your will to that sin's power. Use this time in the shower to train your will to not surrender to the temptation to quit. This is a training we have to do constantly.

DAY 13

"We live in such a way that no one will stumble because of us, and no one will find fault with our ministry. In everything we do, we show that we are true ministers of God. We patiently endure troubles and hardships and calamities of every kind. We have been beaten, been put in prison, faced angry mobs, worked to exhaustion, endured sleepless nights, and gone without food. We prove ourselves by our purity, our understanding, our patience, our kindness, by the Holy Spirit within us, and by our sincere love. We faithfully preach the truth. God's power is working in us. We use the weapons of righteousness in the right hand for attack and the left hand for defense. We serve God whether people honor us or despise us, whether they slander us or praise us."

2 Corinthians 6:3-8a (NLT)

"As you can see, you are reuniting with the parachute bags from your original stay here. Hooyah brothers. The bags will remind us of the light at the end of the tunnel of this dark cold night. We are about to begin a 15-mile walk as a warrior elite team.

"The goal of this walk is to serve as a pillar of remembrance in your mind. We want you to remember the night you surrendered any identity to the darkness you have been controlled by, or identified at time in your life. To serve as a remembrance that your will is unbreakable by the pain in the moment when you walk in the Spirit and with your brothers in Christ.

"Then at the end of this walk, the Founder and I have new Soulcon shirts for you, with one word on the front. We will explain this word more when we get to the finish line, but it's something we spent a lot of time seeking the Holy Spirit about. We believe it will be a word that will help you identify with your new man constantly in your life. Once we reach that point, you will put your new name shirt on, and then we will welcome the sunrise as we jump out of a plane at 11,000 feet. It's our prayer that tonight and tomorrow morning will be a time you never forget, and one that sears into your memory who you are in Christ from this point forward. Let's do this!"

Man, 15 miles? I could go for 15 hours of sleep. With the late night last night, an early start to get to the airport on time and a long travel day, I can feel my flesh wanting to take control of my soul and guide my actions based on the feelings in the moment. I feel a few waves of emotions crashing into my brain, emotions working to get me to doubt. I know what to do in these moments...I just have to do it.

"I can do this. With Christ I am strong, even when I feel weak. With your help Lord I will finish this strong," I say under my breath, as I join the ranks of my team and move forward. I am thankful for the discipline of self-talk, it's helped me tremendously, and I pray it does tonight as well.

All of the sudden I hear a guy start to sing a song. My mind goes back to when Tyler started singing Amazing Grace during our Ice Bath Training. That crazy guy was always one who could look past the pain in the moment. Man, he would love this training... And I know I would love to have him here.

I take a deep breath, and think of honoring Tyler. So I start singing along with the team. As I do that, I slowly start to smile thinking that I am truly ten times stronger than I know. Then I say quietly to the Lord, "Lord Jesus thank you for these men. Help me lean in fully to this challenge. Help me grow in you to the level I never give sin a thought again. Help me be like Jesus. I live to worship you sir. I will worship no matter what. I love you, Lord."

"Not that I was ever in need, for I have learned how to be content with whatever I have. I know how to live on almost nothing or with everything. I have learned the secret of living in every situation, whether it is with a full stomach or empty, with plenty or little. For I can do everything through Christ, who gives me strength."

Philippians 4:11-13 (NLT)

Daily Challenge
Today is the four-minute cold shower day. I want you to picture yourself with this Soulcon Warrior Elite team. In the cold, exhausted, but focused on forging an unbreakable will in Christ. During this time in the shower I pray the Lord does an incredible work in your heart. Think of a few worship songs, and sing them to the Lord. Make a

commitment today that no matter what, no matter how difficult of a challenge you're facing, that you will worship the Lord in the midst of the challenge. He is worthy of our praise…

"Two people are better off than one, for they can help each other succeed. If one person falls, the other can reach out and help. But someone who falls alone is in real trouble. Likewise, two people lying close together can keep each other warm. But how can one be warm alone? A person standing alone can be attacked and defeated, but two can stand back-to-back and conquer. Three are even better, for a triple-braided cord is not easily broken."

Ecclesiastes 4:9-12 (NLT)

It has to be almost sunrise. We've been walking all night and I can feel fatigue throughout my whole body. It feels like, with each step, my body makes a new excuse to quit. I have never been pushed this far, and it's only the morning of the first full day.

"Alright brothers," Bugsly yells out with his usual smile that looks like he loves every bit of this pain we're enduring. "Let's pick up the pace. This is a 15-mile walk, not a crawl. Focus your mind on the end, not the feelings in the moment. We'll have some nice hot coffee when we finish, and a full breakfast."

For whatever reason, that's all I needed to hear. Hot coffee and a full breakfast sounds incredible. I can't wait to chow down. Suddenly the thought comes into my mind about the feeling I had in my stomach the last time I jumped out of a plane with Bugsly. It felt like I was going to puke everywhere. But at this point, fear has absolutely no power over me and I feel like eating a full breakfast would be worth it, even if I puke. And if I hurl, it's aimed right at Bugsly for making us go through this form of hell on day one. I mean I love the guy, but this is brutal.

"Commander Bugsly! What time is it anyway?" I yell out with a voice that surprised me with how weak it sounded.

"It's almost time brother," Bugsly yells back.

Almost time? What kind of answer is that? Almost time for what? Maybe he meant it's almost time for the coffee and the full breakfast.

That would make everything so much better, but I don't think that's it. I can't even see a hint of sunrise yet.

"What an answer!" Alfred says with a voice that sounds just as fatigued as mine. "You just have to love this guy. It seems like both he and the Founder love this stuff a little too much."

"I agree! And man, I am thankful for these guys. I am just a little nervous for what the next event is," I said, as I started to think what they had in store for us, still praying it's the coffee and a really early breakfast.

Our team all saw it at the same time. I remember the first time I heard this river when Tyler and I just arrived at the Training Center, but oddly enough we never saw the river during our stay here. And at that time it would have been nice to see since it was in the middle of summer. Seeing it now just sends even more chills across my body. Surely, there's a bridge...

"Alright brothers. It's time to learn the importance of linking arms together in the face of challenges. Do me a favor, set your bags down and grab a drink of water. I want to share with you something I pray inspires your heart on a deeper level to not walk out of accountability for the remainder of your mission on this earth," the Founder says to our team.

"One of the most important lessons we all need to live and know daily is that WHEN we fall, we need brothers with us to pull us back up. As we all embark on this journey together, we are going to focus our meditations of our heart and mind fully on our identity in Christ, but we CANNOT be ignorant to the weak areas of our flesh. We will teach you from here on out that your flesh has no part in your deep thought life, but it is an enemy that we have to be aware of constantly. This mindset helps all of us to grow in God's grace daily as we become like Christ. But we cannot allow the thought that our sin will be dead for the rest of our lives become a reality. It will always be lurking at the door, waiting to make subtle deathblows to our soul with the fork that feeds our flesh. We just have to stay connected with each other in transparent accountability, so when we fail, we have men around us that can pull us back up and push us toward our identity and not our sin.

"I hope this is sinking in. We want you to be warriors who are elite in Christ, with unbreakable wills in Christ, who fully focus on their mission and calling. But we don't want you to be ignorant to the dangers of your flesh. So we are about to put this into practice. This river is between us and where we need to be at sunrise, which praise God is only about twenty minutes away. But to get to where we need to be we are going to have to walk through something painful.

"This river currently is cold enough that it would take your life if you stayed in it too long, it also has a strong current that would make it dangerous for you to cross by yourself when you're not cold, tired and hungry, but in this fatigued state it is even more dangerous. Brothers, this river is just a symbol of how we need each other as men in this life. There are going to be times when we literally won't be able to make it alone. Where we know we have to walk directly through the pain, when we know there is no other way than to face the threats of this life head on. And in those times, it calls for you to get closer to your brothers than you have ever been. This world teaches that when hard times come, a man can fix the problem by himself, alone, and then move on. This is the antithesis of the Gospel. We need each other daily, and especially when we're facing challenging trials. So let's get our bags back on, and Bugsly will instruct us on how to cross."

Daily Challenge
Do you have brothers like this in your life on a monthly basis? At Soulcon we are so grateful that you're connected to the Soulcon community through our App, but we all need to take it a step further. We need to have coffee face-to-face and eye-to-eye with our Soulcon brothers at least once a month. If you have this praise God. Send your brother or brothers a message today letting them know you're grateful for them. If you don't have this, your challenge before today is over, is to ask a brother for this type of warrior brotherhood. Face-to-face and eye-to-eye relationships are the ones that will help you through the most challenging of times as a warrior of Christ.

WEEK 02 RESULTS AND REFLECTIONS

Be sure to share your results and encourage others going through the challenge on the SOULCON App.

Weekly Objectives

- Hand out five Gospel Tracts each week (You can purchase those from Soulcon.com)
- Live the Soulcon lifestyle with food, this time with no carbohydrates after 1 p.m. – Eat healthy for six days, and have one feast day
- Run, walk or crawl, at least two 5ks (some weeks the runs are longer)
    - o These can also be on an elliptical or bike if your knees won't allow you to run.
- Exercise a total of five days each week for at least 30 minutes each time

Daily Objectives

- Start every day on your knees, praying the Lord's Prayer aloud for your family and your Soulcon brothers.
- Knock out 40 push-ups right after the prayer.
    - o Let your Soulcon Dog Tag hit the ground every time. This is a great reminder that falling down is common, but getting back up is what takes the strength. Also, it's a great reminder for your body that it will obey the goals you have and you will not obey the lusts it has.
- Read the daily devotionals
- Drink one gallon of water every day
- No carbohydrates other than from vegetables, berries and sweet potatoes after 1pm (except on your feast day)

DAY 15

"If you're going through hell, keep going."

Winston Churchill

Reaching down to grab my bag I could feel that my body was growing weary, but nobody else was complaining, so I was going to keep my mouth shut. I grabbed my bag, threw it on my back, and gave Alfred a head nod. I was giving it my all to make that head nod a manly one, I didn't want to show that I would rather sit down, cry and sleep right here than go through this freezing river. I mean it has to be below freezing out here, and we're about to go through this river. What about hypothermia after we get to the other side? What about my parachute getting wet? What if one of us doesn't make it?

While my mind is spinning out of control with anxiety, Bugsly starts to instruct us.

"Right on, right on, brothers! Hooyah! We have one small obstacle between us and hot coffee, full breakfast, and fresh dry clothes. First, I want to congratulate you all on finishing this grueling 15 miles on this cold and sleepless night. Well done men. Now commit in your mind, right where you are to finish strong through this next challenge. This river is going to mess with your mind, but as long as we stay linked together and we don't stop moving, it won't kill our bodies.

"This river is only waist deep, and don't worry, your parachute bag is waterproof, so you're good to go. We all need to just stay focused on one step at a time, and it is imperative that we keep our arms locked together. Do not loosen your grip on your brother's arm for any reason. There are rocks along the river bed that we can get tripped up on, and a current that will have no mercy on even the best swimmer in the group. If we keep moving, step-by-step this should be about 90 seconds of pain. We've got this. Let's go!"

As he finished speaking, we all looked at each other and linked arms, bracing ourselves for the pain. We approached the river like a true special forces group. Then right before we entered the water, we all turned to make sure our chest was facing the current. This would allow us to side step across, helping us to minimize the chance of tripping.

The Founder was in the front of the group, and Bugsly was the last man. The Founder started to lead us into the river. Every man, including myself started to squeal like little kids when the water hit our legs, then step-by-step, we got deeper in the river. And the water came up above our waistline... nobody was laughing. We were all focusing on the next step and keeping our breath. A real sense of fear started to run through my body. But I had to stay focused. I had to.

"Push," Bugsly yelled out. "Don't slow down, don't camp out here in this hell, keep pushing through. We're almost there!"

His words came out of his mouth with strength, but everything in me was panicking. It was only my brothers next to me keeping me moving. Step by freezing cold step we made it!

"Well done m...mm..e...ee..nn!" the Founder slowly stuttered to our team as his body shook from the cold. "Let's get over to the fire and get warmed up and in dry clothes. We made it!"

Wow. What an experience. I have never been in a situation like that. I literally only kept moving forward because of the guys with me. There was nothing in me that could have remained focused if it wasn't for this group with me. Crazy... I know that is a lesson I will never forget. I can never live without brothers around me because I never know when those situations will hit in my life.

Daily Challenge
Fill your bath up with the coldest water possible. And then add all the ice that you can. Your challenge is to work on your mental focus and toughness. Set a timer, and sit down in the water. Make sure the water is above your waist and sit there for 90 seconds. Embrace the joys to be found in this level of suffering today brothers.

DAY 16

"Therefore He says: 'Awake, you who sleep, Arise from the dead, And Christ will give you light.'"

Ephesians 5:14 (NKJV)

Our team started walking toward the fire and the smell of fresh coffee, turkey bacon, eggs and sweet potatoes cooking over the fire filled our shivering, icicle filled nostrils. Praise God! What a glorious smell! As we got closer to the fire we could start to see the clothes around the fire. Thankfully the darkness was starting to break with the rising sun, but we still couldn't see that far in front of our faces. I am sure all the other guys were just as curious as me to find out what name was on the front of our shirts. We all walked over to our dry clothes, and we picked up our shirts.

As I unfold my shirt, I squint my eyes to try to engage focus through the fatigue, and I see the words, HELPER. My hearts starts racing. How did they know? This is a word I have seen throughout my life associated with my name but I have never paused to understand its meaning, because it sounds like the word for a woman. I have always overlooked this word, but today, I believe something is about to shift. I reach down to check out my other gear: cargo pants, cold weather underwear, a warm jacket, warm socks and actual combat boots. Wow!! Without hesitating I strip down and start changing. As I am changing I am surprised that not one guy cracked the "cold water" jokes. But we are all too focused on getting warm, nobody has the energy to bust each other's balls. Probably because everything is in hiding, because that river was so cold.

I put on the last piece of my new gear, and can feel the hope that warmth might be a possibility again soon. It feels like I have been shivering since I got out of the van yesterday.

"Alfred, what name does your shirt have on it?"

"Brother, it's incredible. It says OVERCOMER. I can't even to begin to tell you how much this means to me. When my daughter was in her fight with cancer, there was a song that kept coming on the radio with this word. It felt like every time I needed it the most this song would come on. There is no way they knew that. That is something only the Lord and I know. God is so good!" Alfred says to me with tears in his eyes.

"Praise God! Mine is the same way brother. As you can see, it's HELPER. I haven't even focused on this because I thought it was for women. Since my name can be gender neutral, I thought it was geared toward a woman, but I have seen this with my name so many times in my life. My wife doesn't even know about this. How cool! I can't wait to find out how they got these names for us."

As we are standing there, Commander Bugsly comes up and asks us all to come closer to the fire for the morning meeting before breakfast. We all grab a cup of this incredible smelling coffee and we head over to him, closer to the fire.

"I hope you guys enjoy your new clothes. The Soulcon team spent a lot of time soaking each of you in prayer. We worked to hear from the Lord for a name for each of you. We had your pictures on the wall for a month. We would meet as a team and ask the Lord for guidance, then we discussed what we thought we heard Him speaking to our hearts. Our goal is to get each of you to identify with a new name, even beyond your current name. Please understand, we are just men following a perfect God, so we might have missed hearing from the Lord. But I promise we spent focused time in prayer. So we ask each of you to identify with this name for the remainder of your stay here at Soulcon Warrior Elite Training and we understand that this name might not resonate with your spirit, but we pray it does. We challenge each of you to seek the Holy Spirit and see if this name is a fit for your life. If it is, lock in and never look back.

As we are reflecting on our new names in Christ, I want us each to meditate on the realization that with these names there is nothing of our sinful man. Nothing. If we can each live from our heavenly identity, then we can truly advance the Kingdom by force. We cannot advance God's Kingdom without walking in our new man in His Spirit. So please prepare your heart, and as we watch the sunrise over the horizon, picture your old man dead, completely crucified. Visualize how you are only alive in Christ. That you are a new man, and the old man is gone. Completely. And in that state of visualization, commit your heart to the Lord to never look back into the darkness. Leave it behind you.

Brothers, every lust, every ounce of pride, everything this world offers you. Let it go today...completely. That is not you, the old man has been crucified. It's time to live solely from our new man in the Spirit of God. Let the rising sun represent the darkness being stripped away from your life, to never go back. Let's stay in this place and we will grab breakfast at dawn."

Daily Challenge
Do you have a name from the Lord? If so, share that name with your team. If not, ask the Lord to show your heart a name from His heart for your new man. Then take 5 minutes today and sit out in the sun to practice what the team went through today. Visualize the light of Christ melting away any sin from your life. Visualize what it will be like in heaven to no longer have this tent of flesh that lusts for sins that break God's heart. Let's have a goal to only meditate on our heavenly self from here on out. We have to be aware of our weaknesses, but meditating only on heaven. Love you guys. Proud of you!

DAY 17

"In a wealthy home some utensils are made of gold and silver, and some are made of wood and clay. The expensive utensils are used for special occasions, and the cheap ones are for everyday use. If you keep yourself pure, you will be a special utensil for honorable use. Your life will be clean, and you will be ready for the Master to use you for every good work. Run from anything that stimulates youthful lusts. Instead, pursue righteous living, faithfulness, love, and peace. Enjoy the companionship of those who call on the Lord with pure hearts."
2 Timothy 2:20-22 (NLT)

"Breakfast is ready!" The Founder yells out to us, breaking the silence as each of us were meditating and fighting sleep, as we think on, or dream about, the Lord's grace. "Grab your breakfast and join us back by the fire. Let's get fueled and warm so we can take on the challenges the rest of today."

"Sounds good to me. At this point I finally have empathy for Esau when he sold his birthright for food," I say to Alfred.

"Bro, that's awesome. I hear ya man," Alfred says, as we grab a plate and start loading it with fuel.

It's amazing how good eggs, sweet potatoes, and turkey bacon can smell when you're this hungry. I can't wait to dive in. I have been eating this Soulcon way for a while and have never had a breakfast like this cooked over a fire. This gives me hope that I can make healthy breakfasts on family camping trips. I think my kids would even enjoy this.

Before heading back to sit down I grab another cup of coffee. One of our teammates comes up and starts talking to me,

"Hey man, I'm Nick. I've heard all about you. I go to church with Gage."

"Nick, it's great to meet you bro. I love and miss that guy! How is he doing?"

"So good. He actually got invited to this class, but he is serving as a full-time missionary in the Middle East. Since I was the guy he was discipling, he recommended me to Commander Bugsly for this Warrior Elite Training. You know, it was crazy, I grew up with Gage and he was a typical cookie-cutter Christian. Never rocking the boat and always looking like he had it all together. After he came back from the training center, he turned our men's ministry upside down. It was because of him I experienced freedom from my porn addiction. He was the first guy in my entire life that looked me straight in my eyes and asked me how I was doing with sexual purity. I have been in church my whole life like Gage, and nobody ever talked to me face-to-face about this. When he asked me, I gave him the church answer, and then he asked again. He explained that we're both men, and that if I'm even taking small bites from the fork that feeds my flesh it will slowly destroy my life. And it was at that point that I broke down. For the first time confessing to a brother. I had confessed to the Lord numerous times, but no one else knew, not even my wife. I felt trapped in the sin I never intended to get so addicted to. But it spiraled out of control and I found myself helpless until Gage came along. So I owe him so much respect and gratitude for being bold and direct in the Lord with me. Now my mission is to be that direct with every man I come in contact with inside of the local church with sexual purity. I never believe the fake smile on Sunday morning any more. I look for and pray for opportunities to ask the uncomfortable questions. I don't know where I would be without Gage having the courage to confront me like a warrior."

"Wow. Praise God! That made my day brother. I will make sure I connect with Gage soon to send him encouragement and ask if there's anything they need. I will be praying for them for sure. So do you lead the men's ministry in his place now Nick?"

"Yes sir. Our church is growing stronger than we have ever been in the grace of our Lord Jesus. We are truly a training ground for special forces soldiers for Jesus. That's why I am so thankful I'm here. I want to take my life to the next level in Christ. It's nice to be here with warriors like you brother. I am so grateful. And tired. And hungry." After Nick finished we both had a good laugh thinking about the struggle of fighting to keep our eyelids open and how hungry we are.

"Let's go sit back down brother, chow down on this food and see what Commander and the Founder have in store for us in this next challenge."

As I sit down, my heart fills with pride for the life Gage has lived since he returned from our team. I love that guy and I am so proud of him. I am amazed to see how God worked in all of our lives from that group of men and I look forward to seeing the stories to come from this group of warriors. I just pray we all finish strong...

Daily Challenge
Make sure to ask one guy on your team how they are doing with sexual purity. Make sure it's not in a group setting, but one-on-one. Whether a phone call, text message or an in-person meeting. Reach out and open yourself to hear from them. They might be fighting a struggle they cannot win without confessing to another brother in Christ.

DAY 18

"See then that you walk circumspectly, not as fools but as wise, redeeming the time, because the days are evil. Therefore do not be unwise, but understand what the will of the Lord is."
Ephesians 5:15-17 (NKJV)

After our morning chow and a debrief about our upcoming jump, it's time to board the plane. Again, I find myself with a flood of emotions, but this time there is more excitement than anxiety. I have learned a lot about living a courageous life in Christ since our last jump, and I have come to the conclusion that jumping out of a plane is much easier than handing strangers in my home town a Gospel tract. That can get really uncomfortable, really quick.

"Alright brothers, let's get in!" Bugsly yells to our team.

Our team files in and we take our seats. I have to be honest it's pretty cool to see all of these guys in their boots and cargo pants ready to take action in this extreme discipleship training. As the engines start up, I lean my head back on the cold side of the plane, and rest my eyes.

"Hey bro," Alfred says quietly as he pushes my leg, "stay awake, you don't want to miss out on any of this. We can sleep tonight... hopefully."

"You're right bro, I am here to learn not get caught napping through the lessons," I say back acting tough, but really just wanting some shut-eye.

Man, what I would give for a bed and a few hours of sleep. I pray we get to rest after this jump. My legs are fatigued and my mind is starting to get weak the more time passes.

"Soulcon Warrior Elite brothers," the Founder says as he addresses all of us, "I want each of you to know that we are thankful for you, and that everyone at this Training Center believes that you have a calling to impact your city for the Gospel as an elite warrior in God's Kingdom.

But we brought you out here, and we are at this point today, because we want to see if you believe you have what it takes.

"The Commander and I have seen men go through the Soulcon Training Center and then they go back home, and the fork that feeds the flesh overtakes their life. We do everything we can, we pray, we fight for them, but at the end of the day some of them choose to believe the lies of the Enemy that the fork might actually satisfy. And it breaks my heart every time.

"So on this flight I want to address with you and beg you, to dig deep within yourself and answer the question, 'do I fully believe?' Do you fully believe in your calling? Do you fully believe that God is going to use you to turn this world upside down for His Name?

"I know this question seems elementary to soldiers like you, but what I have found over the years is that it's not elementary. It's the most common reason we see for men getting taken out by the Enemy. Men slowly start to doubt what God called them to. Then they start to doubt if certain sins are really that bad. And then they end up living lives conformed to the patterns of this world thinking they can just live off of Satan's radar. And hear me brothers, that is not possible. Once you are on Satan's radar, he will send everything he has to steal, kill and destroy. He is relentless.

"Therefore, what we need from you is to be honest with yourself. We want this plane ride to be a symbol in your life, of you letting everything in your old man go, never to go back to it. No matter what the sin of the flesh is, it's time to leave it above 11,000 feet. It's time for you to be relentless in your calling, and never look back. Ever."

As the Founder finishes, I know this is where I am supposed to be. Right here. Right now. It's my time to stop leaving one hand holding on to the résumé I built in my flesh. It's time to let go completely and live by faith. To live a life that will inspire my family and others after me to trust in the Lord with their whole heart. More than their savings account, more than their college degree or their social status. It's time to go all in from this point forward.

"We're there brothers!" Bugsly yells out as he is opening the door. "Let's go!"

I lead the men this time, remembering that last time I was the final one to jump with Bugsly. I walk up to the door and Bugsly taps my chest where my new name is, HELPER. I nod to him letting him know that I am willing to give my all for my calling. Then he nods back and gives me a proud smile, and I jump…

"But Jesus told him, 'Anyone who puts a hand to the plow and then looks back is not fit for the Kingdom of God.'"

Luke 9:62 (NLT)

Daily Challenge
Take time today and reflect on this reading. Ask yourself the question the Founder had the guys ask themselves. Ask yourself, "do I truly believe?" If the answer is yes. What in your life do you have to change to reflect your belief? Is it the amount you're giving to the local church and the work of the Gospel around the world? Is it with discipling your family? Is there a lust of the flesh that you have been feeding little bites to? Whatever it is, bring it before the Lord and ask Him to help you. Ask Him to help your actions reflect your faith in Him.

"Do you see what this means—all these pioneers who blazed the way, all these veterans cheering us on? It means we'd better get on with it. Strip down, start running—and never quit! No extra spiritual fat, no parasitic sins. Keep your eyes on Jesus, who both began and finished this race we're in. Study how he did it. Because he never lost sight of where he was headed—that exhilarating finish in and with God—he could put up with anything along the way: Cross, shame, whatever. And now he's there, in the place of honor, right alongside God. When you find yourselves flagging in your faith, go over that story again, item by item, that long litany of hostility he plowed through. That will shoot adrenaline into your souls!"

Hebrews 12:1-2 (MSG)

As the van pulls back on the Training Center grounds, we all have a sense of pride in what we just went through. Everyone on the team made the commitment to live all in for their calling on this earth. To leave everything behind them, and live fully immersed in God's will for our lives. What a powerful moment that was for our team, and for me individually. I cannot wait to see what the Lord has in store for each of us during the remainder of our stay here. I just pray sleep is something in store for all of us relatively soon.

"Alright brothers, head in, and you might want to grab a snack and a cup of coffee. You might need it," Bugsly says to the team.

Wait. What? He's got to be kidding right? Why would we need coffee? We should be winding down from our big victory, and just taking it easy for the rest of the afternoon/evening. I don't think I have any more in the tank to give out.

"Hey man, we've got this," Alfred says as he pats me on the shoulder. "We have more in us than we realize, and we are just getting tested. Let's pass the test."

"Amen brother. I hope the prize for passing this test is sleep," I say back doing my best to be light hearted.

We all walk in and head over to fuel up from HQ for whatever lies ahead of us.

Just as I grab my coffee I see a face on the picture catches my tired eyes, is that Tyler? Emotions flood my heart as I rush over to see if that's his picture. Sure enough. There he is, smiling like always. And I lean in to read his tribute.

"He was such a good man," Bugsly says as he pats me on the shoulder.

"Yes he was…" I say back with a heavy heart.

"His bravery in this life for the Lord has inspired so many Soulcon brothers to live daringly for the Lord. We talk about Tyler in every Soulcon class that comes through. We hope every warrior will have a death song with that much honor." Bugsly says as he rests his hand on my shoulder.

"Wow. I know that means the world to him and his family. Thank you for making such a tribute to one of my closest friends."

"Absolutely brother," Bugsly says as we turn to walk back over for our next challenge briefing.

Sipping my coffee, I think about how living fully in the will of God is going to cause my death song to be one of honor, like Tyler. I know he is standing with the heavenly realm cheering me on in the faith during this process. This thought, and the coffee help me catch a second wind.

As I walk into the room where we're meeting, all of the lights are out, and the room has no windows. I take a big drink, and walk in not sure what we're about to experience.

Daily Challenge
Use each meal today to train your imagination to stay focused on the Heavenly Realm cheering you on. Literally picture yourself eating with the saints that have gone before you. I believe if we could see warriors like King David, Joshua, Samson, Elijah, Paul, and Peter we would live with more motivation and more honor in the everyday tasks ahead of

us. Commit with me to live every day with this mindset to bring honor to Jesus and all the saints who have gone before us.

DAY 20

"Keep watch and pray, so that you will not give in to temptation. For the spirit is willing, but the body is weak!"
Matthew 26:41 (NLT)

"Take a seat brothers," one of the men at the front of the room says to our group. I don't think it's the Founder or Commander, but it's so dark in here I can't make out the face.

"Your next challenge is not going to be easy. Your goal is to pray, in the dark, for one hour straight, without falling asleep. The Founder, Commander and myself will all be watching, and if you fall asleep you will fail this challenge. And if you fail three challenges during your time at Warrior Elite you have to wait a year and then submit an application to try again. So stay focused. This is something we believe every warrior of Christ should practice to put themselves in the shoes of the disciples, to truly experience how your body will wrestle with your spirit. Gentlemen, this is an opportunity that is priceless. You have all done incredible to this point and you will have the opportunity to take on the last challenge for today followed by a healthy dinner, and some much needed rack time. Just do us a favor, and enjoy this process to the best of your ability. I believe the Lord has something wonderful in store for you during this time.

"At your desk there is a microphone. During this challenge we want each of you praying out loud for the hour. Learn the power of your words in prayer, and commit to not fall asleep. I hope you had a cup of coffee, this hour might seem like an entire night. But we believe in you guys, so stay alert. I am going to read this passage before we begin to fix our hearts on the importance of this next hour. Kick butt brothers…

Then Jesus went with them to the olive grove called Gethsemane, and he said, "Sit here while I go over there to pray." He took Peter and Zebedee's two sons, James and John, and he became anguished and distressed. He told them, "My soul is crushed with grief to the point of death. Stay here and keep watch with me." He went on a little farther and bowed with his face to the ground, praying, "My Father!

If it is possible, let this cup of suffering be taken away from me. Yet I want your will to be done, not mine." Then he returned to the disciples and found them asleep. He said to Peter, "Couldn't you watch with me even one hour? Keep watch and pray, so that you will not give in to temptation. For the spirit is willing, but the body is weak!" Then Jesus left them a second time and prayed, "My Father! If this cup cannot be taken away unless I drink it, your will be done." When he returned to them again, he found them sleeping, for they couldn't keep their eyes open.

So he went to pray a third time, saying the same things again. Then he came to the disciples and said, "Go ahead and sleep. Have your rest. But look—the time has come. The Son of Man is betrayed into the hands of sinners. Up, let's be going. Look, my betrayer is here!" Matthew 26:36-46 (NLT)

As this man finished reading he turned to walk out of the room. I literally can't see anyone, but I reach out on my desk and grab my microphone. I don't think I have ever prayed out loud for longer than five minutes in my life when I am alert and full of energy. Now I face an hour, sitting here in the dark when I feel like the next blink of my eyes could catch my soul captive into a deep sleep. I have to do this, I have to finish.

"We will begin in three, two, one." The man's voice called out over the speakers in the room.

Here we go… Our whole team starts praying out loud. It actually sounds really cool. I am so thankful to be in this brotherhood. I start to use my imagination to picture myself with the disciples praying in the Garden of Gethsemane and I think of the honor it would have been to be there with Jesus. And then,the focus of my prayers shift. My heart fills with praise to Jesus, and in the middle of my exhaustion His presence fills my body. I start singing praise to Him that is from my heart in my own words. My mind fixates on the majesty of Jesus and who He is. I have never experienced this in prayer before… My mind and heart are fully engaged, and I feel like I don't ever want to leave this place…

"Congratulations men, you all passed with flying colors," the instructor says, as he turns the lights on and about blinds all of us.

I reach over and give Nick and Alfred a high five. Then Nick leans over to me an Alfred and says, "Hey brother, you know that song you were singing?"

"Yeah man," I say back excited to hear what he has to say.

"Can you sing that ten-or?" Nick says back.

"What do you mean?" I ask curiously as I know nothing about music.

"Ten or fifteen miles away. I know it was worshipful to God's heart, but not to my ear drums."

"Punk!" I say as I reach over and punch him on his arm.

"Good one bro," Alfred says as we all get a good laugh.

Daily Challenge

Take 5 minutes today and pray out loud the entire time. Set a timer, and have a goal to not stop speaking or singing to God's heart the entire time. Use your mind and your heart to picture standing in the throne room of God like Isaiah in Isaiah chapter six. Be fully engaged and don't let distraction in. Kick butt brothers.

DAY 21

"I've told you these things for a purpose: that my joy might be your joy, and your joy wholly mature. This is my command: Love one another the way I loved you. This is the very best way to love. Put your life on the line for your friends. You are my friends when you do the things I command you. I'm no longer calling you servants because servants don't understand what their master is thinking and planning. No, I've named you friends because I've let you in on everything I've heard from the Father."

John 15:11-15 (MSG)

"Grab a drink of water brothers," the man with Commander and the Founder says to our team as he breaks up our laughter from the team giving me a hard time for my lack of musical ability.

"Meet us out at the Grinder brothers. Our first team run is waiting for us," Bugsly says with excitement in his voice like we are all kids about to go on our first field trip.

"How is the guy not worn out?" I say to Alfred.

"I hear ya brother, this is a little crazy," Alfred says back, for the first time showing exhaustion in his countenance.

"Keep your chin up brother, we've got this. Don't allow your mind to go down that road. Before we know it this run will be over and we'll be eating." I say back doing my best to channel my inner positive Tyler. "Thanks bro. Love ya man," Alfred says back as he puts his arm around my shoulders, "let's do this."

"This is it, your last challenge of the most difficult day here at the Training Center. Our goal, to finish a 10k as a team. We are going to run at the pace of the slowest guy's pace on the team. We hope and pray this event forges your wills to become unbreakable in Christ. Just stay focused on the goal, and don't give up. We understand your body is aching, your stomachs are hungry and you're ready for bed. The Founder and I are right there with you. But we need you to push through and experience a new level of dependency on the Holy Spirit," Bugsly says to the team.

"Hooyah Bugsly!" I yell back as our team begins to jog together.

As we embark on this journey together, I find myself right next to Alfred again. I will never forget our first team run at the Soulcon Training Center with our original team. I was so frustrated with Alfred when he stopped running and I was judging him for being so overweight. Now look at him, he is the fittest one on our team. This guy is a beast. I am thankful the Lord did that work in my heart then. I have lived committed to live a life that believes the best in others and it has changed my marriage, and every friendship I have. God is so merciful.

Well we're doing it. We have a half-mile left and everyone is still together and jogging as one team. I am amazed that we are pushing past the level of exhaustion our bodies are in.

"Man down, team!" Bugsly yells out.

We all stop in a panicked state. I scan through the team to see who it is. I jog up and see the other instructor laying on the ground. Great, another challenge.

"One of the most important things we can instill into your hearts brothers is to never, at any point, ever, leave a man behind, no matter what it costs you. If you have a brother running with you for almost the entire race, and he falls, most men today in the world will just keep running to make sure they finish their race. All the while they are neglecting the opportunity to be the Good Samaritan to one of their brothers. Please hear me brothers, if you finish strong alone in this life you did not finish strong at all. We need each other, there are going to be times when each of us fall, we cannot leave anyone behind. We have to reach down and pick them up, because if we don't who will? They might just stay where they are and the warriors have all left them to rot and die in their failure. This cannot be, brothers. So this last part of the run is going to be difficult, but engage your heart and mind, and forge your will to always get out of your comfort-zone to grab your brothers when they fall. Your last mission is to carry Instructor Levi back to HQ. After that, it's time for dinner and rack time. Finish strong together brothers."

"We've got this guys!" Alfred says as we pick up Instructor Levi and head back to HQ to finish strong…together.

Daily Challenge
Make sure your 10k is complete before the day ends. I know you might have knocked it out earlier this week, but today is your last day to knock it out. You've got this! And for the challenge for today, ask the Lord if there is someone who has been left behind in your life. Maybe by the local church, by your men's group, or by you personally. Once that person comes to mind, pray for them. Then take action with that prayer. Do your best to connect with them to check in on them. They might be laying in the same place they got left behind, and you reaching out to them might be the hand they need to get back in the fight as a soldier for Jesus Christ.

WEEK 03 RESULTS AND REFLECTIONS

Be sure to share your results and encourage others
going through the challenge on the SOULCON App.

Weekly Objectives

- Hand out five Gospel Tracts each week (You can purchase those from Soulcon.com)
- Live the Soulcon lifestyle with food, this time with no carbohydrates after 1 p.m. – Eat healthy for six days, and have one feast day
- Run, walk or crawl, at least two 5ks (some weeks the runs are longer)
  - These can also be on an elliptical or bike if your knees won't allow you to run.
- Exercise a total of five days each week for at least 30 minutes each time

Daily Objectives

- Start every day on your knees, praying the Lord's Prayer aloud for your family and your Soulcon brothers.
- Knock out 40 push-ups right after the prayer.
  - Let your Soulcon Dog Tag hit the ground every time. This is a great reminder that falling down is common, but getting back up is what takes the strength. Also, it's a great reminder for your body that it will obey the goals you have and you will not obey the lusts it has.
- Read the daily devotionals
- Drink one gallon of water every day
- No carbohydrates other than from vegetables, berries and sweet potatoes after 1pm (except on your feast day)

DAY 22

"And do not be drunk with wine, in which is dissipation; but be filled with the Spirit, speaking to one another in psalms and hymns and spiritual songs, singing and making melody in your heart to the Lord, giving thanks always for all things to God the Father in the name of our Lord Jesus Christ, submitting to one another in the fear of God."

Ephesians 5:18-21 (NKJV)

Rolling out of bed this morning was an interesting experience. It felt like I just blinked my eyes then the alarm was going off. I don't think anyone on the team moved at all during the ten hours of rack time we had. And it was really hilarious; I think all of us forgot what 0430 feels like, especially with legs so sore we could barely stand up. How I've missed this place.

Now our team is gathered for our first meeting, the sun isn't up yet. Here we are again, freezing our butts off sipping this incredible cup of coffee.

"Good morning brothers!" Instructor Levi shouts out to our team.

"Hooyah sir," a few of us shout back to him.

"It's my honor to come alongside Commander and the Founder to be an instructor at this great Training Center. I look forward to helping them push each of you to your limit and then God willing, ten times further. But before we go on, I need to share with you guys why I was the man who went down on our run, and why I'm on the Soulcon staff.

"It was about two years ago when I first came through this training. I am sure like each of you, the Lord did a work in my heart that completely changed every part of my life. At that point in my life, I was someone who went to church occasionally with my family, but most of the time I would rather be working on a project in my garage. My wife would constantly ask me to step up and lead spiritually in our home, but I had no idea how to do it. The only men that I ran into on

Sunday mornings had on a tie and a big smile and I couldn't relate to them at all. I am an ex-special forces soldier like Bugsly, and I was extremely rough around the edges when I would go to church on an occasional basis with my family. So the last thing I wanted was to talk to guys that seemed fake and putting on a show. I had no idea the Enemy was using my judgments about these men as a tool to get me to eat from the fork that feeds my flesh. And that fork for me was alcohol. I never thought it was a problem. My wife and kids would go to bed, and I would go out in the garage to work on different projects I had going for friends and around the house. Before I knew it I was having a six-pack every night.

"Then one morning after my wife got home from church with the kids, she handed me a flyer for Soulcon. I have to say it was the first time I was ever interested in a Christian activity. All of the language on the flyer drew my heart in and I signed up.

"When I walked on the Soulcon grounds, I had no idea what the Lord had in store for my life. For the first time I felt close to the Holy Spirit, and like I could be a true warrior as a Christian. Then Commander and I hit it off, and it was during that six weeks when I laid my addiction to alcohol at the feet of Jesus. It was incredible. Then after graduation, I went home, and became the man God had predestined me to be. I truly was in His perfect will for my life. And then it happened…

"I slowly started to believe that I was a good person. I started to believe in the praise of the people in my local church and community. I had no idea that pride was causing me to drift away from my intimacy with the Lord. But it happened. Before I knew it I was back out in the garage, just having one beer with a project. And the project was a good project, it was for the local church we were attending. The Enemy had me right where he wanted me and I fell. I fell so hard I even started putting alcohol in my coffee when no one was looking. My addiction came back stronger than before, and I was pinned down. I thought I was hiding it from everyone, but people started to notice. So I pulled away. I literally made excuses to get out of every bit of accountability I had at that point. And the crazy thing was that none of my brothers were coming to get me. I was laying right where I fell, and my brothers in the church were just going to keep running their race and leave me to rot and die.

"Then, my wife sent a message to the Commander. He actually flew out to my house. He scared the hell out of me...sorry for the language, but he did. He came into the garage I was in and caught me red handed. He reached into the pit of hell where I was and pulled me out. He saved my life. If it wasn't for him sacrificing his time and a part of his life, I fully believe I would have ended my life in that garage.

"Now I stand before you a living testimony of how we can never leave a man behind. Ever. We have to be willing to storm the gates of hell for our brothers who might fall back into their addictions, just as much as we storm the gates of hell for the lost. We can never lose sight of the importance of getting connected to warriors for Christ, and staying connected to our brothers in Christ."

Daily Challenge

Take time today and sit before the Lord. Force your mind and heart to never believe in the praise of people around you. Force your soul to only find value in Christ alone. Commit to only be focused to bring Christ glory, and no part of you. This seems simple, but you and I both know, the fork-sized bites of the pride of this life are some of the most dangerous. And on the other side of any bite of the fork, is death lurking. We have to run from sin and cling to the Lord and the brotherhood.

DAY 23

"As iron sharpens iron, so one person sharpens another."
Proverbs 27:17 (NIV)

"I want you guys to do me a favor, look at the brother to your right. Then look at the brother to your left. These are not only men you're looking at, but generations of people. We cannot give up on each other men, no matter how dark the sin," Instructor Levi says as he shares with our team while he continues the morning lectures with tears in his eyes.

"Once Commander came and pulled me from the pit of hell I fell into one fork sized bite at a time, I had a lot of work to do, and Commander helped me through that process. He didn't just come and call me out and then leave me. He made the decision to not leave me behind, and then he made the decision to disciple me. He walked through some of the darkest sins in my life to help me realize who I was in Christ. He was firm with me, and at the same time had such patience with me as I developed into the man God created me to be…again.

"What we have today in most churches when a man falls away from close brotherhood is such a weak accountability system that nobody knows he fell, and brothers, that has to change. We cannot have men fall into sin and have nobody in their life to pull them back up, nobody to even know they fell. We have to be the change agents with this brothers. We believe you are here because you are warrior leaders. We understand the average man will complain about their church not having the systems in place to keep their men accountable, but a warrior will find a way to make it happen.

"I believe my mission, from here on out, is to inspire this level of discipleship community inside of the local church. So that's why I am here, and that's my area of focus on the Soulcon Staff Team. I have made a commitment to myself that I will stop at nothing to get men focused on reaching into the pit, and pulling their brothers out when they fall. As men we have to keep our minds sober and alert to constantly be looking out for the attack of the Enemy on our lives, our families' lives, and our brothers' lives. We cannot just focus on our race, or we run the risk of finishing this life alone, and like Commander said, finishing alone is not finishing strong.

"As we go through the day today, we are going to make this very practical within this team. We believe that every warrior brother needs to know at least three things about each brother in their life. The first is their brother's calling in Christ. That's why each of you has a shirt with your name on the front that we prayed through. We think this should be the first identifier in every men's meeting in your churches. This is more important than their job title or work history. The second is the biggest struggle with the flesh their brother has. Finally, the passion they have in their heart that they believe is their responsibility to steward into reality in this world from the heart of God. We believe once you know these three things about a man you will have the tools to keep them accountable to stay in close relationship with the Spirit, and ensure they have little to no room to start destroying their life by walking in the flesh.

"Your mission today is to find one guy on this team that you don't know, and go over these three things during breakfast today."

Daily Challenge
Share these three things with your team today. Share your calling in Christ, your biggest struggle with your flesh, and finally the passion you have in your heart that you believe you are responsible to steward into reality in this world from the heart of God. Then make sure you read what the different men on your team share so you can hold them accountable on this level as you progress through this challenge.

DAY 24

"He must become greater; I must become less."
John 3:30 (NIV)

What a day. Even though we didn't have many physical challenges today, we took a deep dive into growing in relationships with our brothers in Christ. I am amazed how much you can learn about another man by just covering the three main questions Instructor Levi shared with us. I feel like I know my new warrior brother, Caleb, that I just met, better than I know some of the guys I do life with in my home church. It really opened my eyes to how shallow some of my conversations can be even as a man who lives a special forces life for Jesus. This is something that needs changing quickly when I get back home. If we don't know each other this intimately we will slowly become more susceptible to the Enemy's attacks.

"Hey bro," Caleb says in a whisper as some of the guys on the team are sleeping after a long day.

"What's up?" I say back speaking as quietly as possible.

"Thanks for talking with me today man. I hate to admit this, but I haven't talked with another man that openly in a long time. It seems like ever since I became a pastor, people don't ask me questions like that. I guess they assume I have it all together, and I believe that assumption is my own doing. I have implemented Soulcon in a big way in our church, and I see men's lives impacted constantly by this program, but I have slowly stepped out of the trenches of Soulcon with our men. That was never the intention I set out for, but I got there quickly without realizing it. After I personally went through the Training Center it seemed like everything changed for me. I went back to the church, I pastored thinking I could be just one of the guys in the trenches. I longed for the trenches, longed to be one of the guys, but as the pastor found myself leading the organization of the Soulcon groups and encouraging the guys to follow through without ever getting myself transparently connected with the men. I intended to many times, but it never came to fruition. It seemed like one project after another started popping up that as the pastor I had to address and take care of. I didn't even realize that I was slowly doing what King David had done to himself. I was slowly starting to live as the leader removed from the battlefield, and not out in the battlefield with my men. I need to get back to that, I need to be the venerable warrior I once was. The warrior that lived boldly for the Lord and didn't care what people thought about me. I mean, I used to be like David in his prime…completely unashamed in my relationship with the Lord. Now I feel like I am trying to put up a front like I have it all together so the people in my church don't find a reason to lose trust in me. I know that's a lie, but it's the weakness of my flesh we talked about today. I need to find full confidence in Christ, and not the position I currently hold. Today helped me remember that it's not my perfect actions but my passionate, unashamed pursuit of the Lord that inspires the people around me to grow close to the Lord. So, I need to get back to that. More of Christ, and less of me. Thank you, brother. Today meant more to my life and ministry than you know."

"You bet man. I am beyond thankful the Lord brought us together. I look forward to developing a relationship with you and being in your corner through the peaks and valleys ahead bro."

We fist bump, then he turns back to go to bed, and I crawl into my bed. What a great day…

Daily Challenge
Send your pastor an encouraging message today and spend a few minutes praying for him and his family. The position of pastor comes with a lot of stress, a lot of responsibility and at times a lot of isolation. Your message might be the encouragement he needs today.

DAY 25

"Seek the Kingdom of God above all else, and live righteously, and he will give you everything you need."

Matthew 6:33 (NLT)

Hearing the loud scream of the alarm wake our team up would give most of us a heart attack if we weren't in such good shape. It's an interesting thing to wake up at the same time as eleven other men before daybreak.

"Good morning brother!" Nick says as he jumps off the top bunk and heads to the restroom.

How in the world was he able to jump from the top bunk? Are his legs not sore? Mine are killing me.

"Morning bro," I say back, well past the point where he could hear me.

I slowly roll out of bed to get ready to meet over at HQ. All I can think of is a cup of that fresh coffee. My body is so fatigued I might just snort the beans this morning.

"Hey guys," Alfred shouts out to the team, "let's all meet in the middle and do our push-ups and say the Lord's prayer together. I couldn't think of a better way to start the day with you guys."

"Hooyah brother," I say as we all walk toward the middle to start knocking out our push-ups. "Alfred, will you count them out for us?" "I'd be honored." Alfred says as he starts leading us in our 40 push-ups.

I must admit this is pretty cool. Starting my day with eleven other warriors around me each morning would make sticking to a morning routine much easier back home. The lure of hitting the snooze button gets too tempting at times to be able to resist. It would be so much easier with these guys around…and this horrifically loud alarm.

"Well done brothers," Alfred says as we finish the 40th push-up. It's mind-blowing to think where this guy came from. I couldn't be more honored to be his brother in the Lord.

"Hey guys," Caleb says to the group, "before we start our prayer I want to share something with each of you. Yesterday was profound to me and I want to encourage each of you with what the Lord was stirring in my heart last night after lights out.

"If you guys don't know I'm a pastor, and I count it an honor to serve in the Body in this way. But I believe I was doing something all of us could become victim to very easily. I left the Training Center after the six-week experience and I went back home on fire to lead the men in our church. When I got home I was eager to empower men and establish systems for implementing Soulcon at our church. Then the craziness of life caught up, and I started to trust in the systems that I had set in place rather than the Holy Spirit. I did this with my leadership of Soulcon in our men's ministry in our church, and embarrassingly, I did it with my devotion time with the Lord a lot. I would just go through the motions. I wasn't leading to experience the Holy Spirit, I was leading to micromanage the Holy Spirit so I could accomplish every bullet point on my list of objectives. And man, what a scary place to be. I personally believe that place, of what I call living a, 'systems run life' to accomplish the objectives without having a heart connection to the Lord is a place I believe every leader can get caught in. So please hear me, do the daily disciplines, I thank God for the Soulcon lifestyle, but make sure you never leave your passion in bed. Engage your heart in every task and ask the Lord to give you an experience throughout the day with Him. Never let your relationship with God turn into what you and your systems can accomplish. It always needs to be about what He can accomplish through you as He leads you. This is something I need to repent of and confess today. I am done living this way. I commit today to implement this change in my life as of right now."

"Amen. Good word Caleb, thank you for sharing brother. I know that's something we all need to hear. I look forward to experiencing the presence of the Holy Spirit with each of you today," I say as we all get on our knees to go before the Lord and pray the Lord's Prayer.

Daily Challenge

Ask the Lord to search your heart today to make sure you're attentive to His presence more than accomplishing the list of objectives for the day. Our goal as warriors of Christ should be to stay connected to the Holy Spirit every second for the rest of our lives. We know there is a war for our connection with the Lord and we have to fight to experience His presence daily. It's worth the fight. Stay focused and connected brothers.

DAY 26

"I have hidden your word in my heart, that I might not sin against you."

Psalm 119:11 (NLT)

As we walk into the classroom for our morning meeting, I can feel the soreness starting to lessen in my legs. This is great, I know they only took it easy on us yesterday because of the beatings our bodies endured during the first, never ending day.

"Morning warriors," Bugsy yells out to the class. "Take your seats and let's get started!"

How I've missed a cup of black coffee in my hand and the sound of that guy's voice. It's like a calming peace and a warning before the storm, all at the same time.

"I hope everyone is rested and fueled up for the challenges that are ahead of us today. We don't want to miss out on experiencing the fullness God has for us in this life because of lack of stewardship of these bodies. Our goal with these bodies at Soulcon is to push our bodies to the limit to be as healthy as possible, so we can focus on the most important thing, making Jesus known to this hurting world. "This is what we are going to deep dive into today, this topic is of upmost importance. Your first time through you all did incredible, but now it's time. It's time to take it to the point of no return. One of the things we have found is some of our Soulcon brothers went through the six-week program, and then fell back into their old lifestyle after they were done. We know this is possible for all of us, but the more we know who we are in Christ, the less we lust for things of this world, and that's our mission this time around.

"Each one of you has your name on the front of your Soulcon Warrior Elite shirts. Our goal is to help you line up every action, deep thought, and emotion with your new identity in Christ. What we put on your shirts is soaked in prayer from us, but if that word is not spot on for you, we challenge you to go before the Lord. Ask Him to reveal to you a name that could help identity you. Maybe it's encourager, maybe unbreakable, maybe rock, maybe pillar, whatever it is it will be personal between you and the Lord. Just like taking personality tests, this is a spiritual identity test before the Lord we all need to take. Once we know our identity, no doubt can have authority over our lives. We have too many people in this world fighting to believe in who they are, they are constantly looking for things, events, and successes to identify them. Brothers, this cannot be us. If we allow this to happen, we will be deceived. If our identity is in Christ, no success or failure will distract us from completing our mission from the Lord at the highest level possible.

"As you have heard, this time through, failure in this program is a possibility. We want to do our best to see if you can push through some of the most difficult challenges we can dish out to help you focus on your identity more than the feelings and thoughts you will have in the moment. So along with the challenges we will have for you here, each of you will be challenged to memorize Ephesians 5:1-21 and recite it to one of the instructors on your final day here. Along with this, you will have to pass the breath hold test. This is where you have to hold your breath for 90 seconds."

Wait what? What in the world does holding my breath have to do with my relationship with the Lord? I don't know what to think about this one, but I'll give it a shot. I trust these guys have all of our best interests in mind.

"Now, I am sure this might be overwhelming for some of you to hear. But please hear me, you can do it if you focus. We believe in you. We have to get back to the point where men are constantly being challenged in their relationship with the Lord. Scripture memorization cannot be a lost art brothers, we have to restore the importance of memorizing and reciting God's Holy Word. Also, we can never stop pushing our bodies to the next level to develop our mind and emotions in Christ. Our goal by doing this is to forge a will that is completely unbreakable in our walk with the Holy Spirit. If the Enemy can get you to practice surrendering your will to a cupcake, more than likely he can get you to surrender your will to quitting on your marriage, viewing porn, giving in to your lust for alcohol, or any other major sin in your life. Please remember what we teach at Soulcon, every sin is equal in God's eyes, but not every sin has equal consequences in these mortal bodies. James 4:17 paints a clear picture of what sin is,

'Remember, it is sin to know what you ought to do and then not do it.' (NLT)

"If you know you're not supposed to eat a cupcake, and you do it anyway, that's sin in God's eyes. But we all know that each sin has a different consequence in this life. Just like if you get tempted to cheat on your wife, and you act on it. Or if you get angry with someone and you take their life. Both of these extreme examples are sin as well, but during our stay on this earth they have different consequences than other sins. The incredible news we all know and live in, is that every sin was forgiven completely on the cross. It's our job to walk in righteousness and not sin. Our mindset has to be clearly focused on following Jesus and not our lusts. Brothers, we cannot use God's grace as an excuse to sin. We have to stay committed to walk in His grace to live in righteousness through faith and obedience. It's imperative that we remember that faith without works is dead, and we are not training baby Christians in this program, we are training Soulcon Warriors to live elite lives in Christ Jesus every second for the rest of their lives. So, what we are going to cover during the remainder of your time might offend you, honestly some of it might anger you, but you have two options, either you accept the challenge or you walk away. We are looking for the guys who will lean into the challenge and give up everything to sprint after Jesus with as much energy as possible."

Daily Challenge
Take today and reflect on your life to this point. Ask the Lord to help you push through to the next level. My goal in writing this is to inspire your heart to walk fully in faith and obedience with the Lord. Like Dietrich Bonhoeffer, I hate the message of cheap grace. The grace that was given to us on the cross cost Jesus everything. Actually, as I am writing this day, it is 4:50am and I am sitting next to the Sea of Galilee. I have been overwhelmed with the emotion of how much Jesus truly gave so we could live. So brothers, we have to give our all for Him... we have to. Yes, He will love us unconditionally no matter what, but please let's follow Him with 100% intensity, in His grace, every day. Love you guys. I pray you experience the Lord in a new way today, and that you leave any sin in your life at the cross, never to pick it up again.

DAY 27

"If you always put limit on everything you do, physical or anything else. It will spread into your work and into your life. There are no limits. There are only plateaus, and you must not stay there, you must go beyond them."

Bruce Lee

"Here is what I want you to do, scan your life and ask the Lord what weight you're carrying that you don't need to be. Right now, in your seats, ask Him. We are going to continue with this lecture, but I want you to focus on never losing your internal dialogue with the Lord. He knows areas that are weighing us down, that we are unaware of, and I believe He is constantly waiting to reveal those to us if we would just slow down and listen to Him. We need to be in God's peace in any situation in this life, and that's why we will push you to memorize these verses and practice holding your breath.

"I know most of you overachievers are wondering why we are not just memorizing the entire fifth chapter of Ephesians. Well, I have great news, and hopefully a great motivator for you. If you pass this course, you will earn a paid trip back with no registration fee for you and your wife for the Soulcon Marriage, four day intensive. At that point you both will memorize the remainder of that chapter."

Wow. That is so cool! My wife would be thrilled! She has always said how badly she wants to experience the training and teaching of this program, and now, if I can pass these two weeks, we can have a chance to go through this together! How cool. I better lock in and stay focused.

"We would love to meet your wives and help you all navigate through building the strongest marriage possible in Christ. But before then, and you guys know this, we have to focus on the strength of you. A man is the head of his wife, so we have to make sure you as the head remain sober and alert. That's our mission, and we will exhaust our lives to complete this mission the Lord Jesus has assigned us.

"As for the breath holding, this is one of the most practical ways to push your mind to the next level and start training your will not to give in when you feel temptation. During the 90 seconds you will feel signals of panic that are all false. Your brain will try to tell you what to do, because it only thinks in the natural. You have to override it for a supernatural training. During this time we want you to picture yourself breathing in the spirit, sitting peacefully inside your body in the middle of a self-induced storm. You can do it brothers.

"We want you to start practicing these two objectives today. You don't have the full six weeks here like before, you only have until graduation day to complete these two tasks. Also, there will be a few more challenges that are new that are on a pass or fail grade scale. Just do your best and give 100%... and then 10 times more. Take a break and we are going to come back in and hear from one of my good friends, a Soulcon graduate and an ultra-marathon runner on the importance of understanding your pace in different seasons of life."

Daily Challenge

Let your team know how you're doing with your breath holding challenge as well as your challenge to memorize Ephesians 5:1-21. To graduate from this program and earn the opportunity to purchase the Warrior Elite Dog Tag, these are two objectives that you have to complete. There is no room for failure here brothers. Give this your all, and then ten times more. Love you guys, and thankful for each of you. The harvest in this world is truly plentiful, I am thankful you have answered the call to be the few.

DAY 28

"The only limit to our realization of tomorrow will be our doubts of today."

Franklin D. Roosevelt

"Hey Alfred," I yell out as we all stand up for a coffee break, "wait up!"

"Can you believe it brother? If we pass our wives get to come! Talk about motivation…my wife has wanted to come to this Training Center ever since I came back. She is going to be so excited."

"I hear ya brother," Alfred says back as he lets out a big sigh. "I need to pass this course big time so my wife can come. This is a big answer to prayer for me. I just don't know how to lead in this area with her, and I think she just needs to experience this process. And how cool, we could do it together for Soulcon Marriage. I am stoked."

"Now, we just need to pass, right?" I say back jokingly, but honestly I don't think I have ever memorized more than two verses consecutively in my life. This is going to push me big time. Not even to mention holding my breath for 90 seconds. That sounds impossible. But with the possibility of my wife being able to come through this training on the line, I will do what I need to. I look forward to what the Lord has for me on the other side of this testing.

Alfred and I grab our coffee and head back into the classroom. Both of us are uneasy about the difficulty of the challenges ahead of us, but charged up with a new motivation, to get our wives here.

"Hopefully this guy can teach us something about working on our mental focus to finish since he enjoys running 100 miles without stopping!" I say, as we both grab our chairs.

"Good morning my Soulcon brothers!" says the man who must be the ultra-marathoner to our team. "I hope you're all doing great! It is my honor and privilege to be here with you today. I hope what the Lord has placed on my heart will bless your soul in a way it hasn't been ministered to before. I pray that any time before I speak to men, because I know we serve a God who is capable of just that. We serve a God who never runs dry, and who longs to fill us anew every day, and I pray this is that for your soul.

"As the Commander said, I am both a Soulcon graduate as well as someone who runs ultra-marathons, and that is why I am here to share with you. I want to impart what I've learned from the 100-mile races with each of you just in case you never have the opportunity to run one. I know that distance is not for everyone, but let me tell you, pushing yourself with your cardiovascular health is for everyone. And before I dive in, I have to tell you that I am proud of you guys for taking the opportunity to be at this Warrior Elite training. I believe God has great things in store for each of you if you remain 100% present in the Spirit and live with 100% intensity every day. And that is a great segue into what I have to share with you guys.

"As I was seeking the Lord as to what to share, I felt that He placed the word *pace* on my heart. When I believe I heard this from Him, I got excited and knew exactly what I wanted to share. You see pace is something that is very important for runners, and especially ultra-marathon runners. When a runner sets out on a run, they want to average a certain pace the entire time. That's their goal, and should be a goal for each of us. But one thing a runner doesn't do, is they don't expect to run that pace through the entire race. Their goal is to average that pace. Every runner knows there are going to be uphill times of the run as well as downhill. There will also be times when the wind is in your face and when the wind is at your back. There are so many variables runners have to deal with and factor into the run they are setting out for. But just because a runner has to slow their pace down on a hill doesn't mean they get discouraged and quit, they understand there will be these slower times where your pace slows down, but they also understand with every uphill there is a downhill coming. Then on the downhill we can make up some time on the run.

"I believe the reason I am here is to encourage you as a warrior for Christ, that you have to start looking at the pace of your life, like a runner does for the pace of their run. You cannot lose hope during the uphill times brothers. You just have to shorten your stride and be okay with a slower pace during that time. But when the uphill is over and you hit an easier point in your life as a follower of Jesus, don't sit back and become lazy. You must make up some of that time from the uphill. Every day God has different challenges in store for you. Some are flat surface challenges, some are uphill, some downhill, some with the wind right in your face, and some with the wind kicking behind you. No matter what, you must push hard in the everyday. You have to keep focused on the finish of your ultra-marathon life. Your goal should be to finish with the fastest overall pace possible for your ability, never making excuses to slow down. You guys know as well as I do, this world needs men who are growing in their intensity in the Lord moment by moment. This world needs all of us to be warriors.

"Therefore, during every run, focus on your pace. I pray you always remember what I shared with you. No matter what you're facing, push to keep your average pace focused on finishing strong. I love and appreciate you guys, and I know your next challenge is a big one. I am going to do it with you! We are going to head out for the timed seven-mile run. I believe in you guys. Let's see what we're capable of in Christ."

Wait. What did he just say? A seven-mile run? Dang. My legs are finally not painfully sore from the incredibly long first day of festivities… oh well, bring it on.

Daily Challenge
On your seven-mile run today, focus on your average pace. Learn the lessons from the hills, the winds and any other external challenge along the way, but do your best to finish with the average pace you set out for. Love you guys. Proud of you! Kick butt today and leave it all on the field! Hooyah.

WEEK 04 RESULTS AND REFLECTIONS

Be sure to share your results and encourage others
going through the challenge on the SOULCON App.

Weekly Objectives

- Hand out five Gospel Tracts each week (You can purchase those from Soulcon.com)
- Live the Soulcon lifestyle with food, this time with no carbohydrates after 1 p.m. – Eat healthy for six days, and have one feast day
- Run, walk or crawl, at least two 5ks (some weeks the runs are longer)
    - o These can also be on an elliptical or bike if your knees won't allow you to run.
- Exercise a total of five days each week for at least 30 minutes each time

Daily Objectives

- Start every day on your knees, praying the Lord's Prayer aloud for your family and your Soulcon brothers.
- Knock out 40 push-ups right after the prayer.
    - o Let your Soulcon Dog Tag hit the ground every time. This is a great reminder that falling down is common, but getting back up is what takes the strength. Also, it's a great reminder for your body that it will obey the goals you have and you will not obey the lusts it has.
- Read the daily devotionals
- Drink one gallon of water every day
- No carbohydrates other than from vegetables, berries and sweet potatoes after 1pm (except on your feast day)

DAY 29

"In your strength I can crush an army; with my God I can scale any wall."

Psalm 18:29 (NLT)

As we get to where we're about to start our seven-mile run, Commander Bugsly begins to share with the team.

"Alright gentlemen, let's make sure your boots are tied tight and have a double knot. We don't want any distractions. This event is a test to see if you will give 100% intensity to the level you're capable of. The Founder and myself have a spreadsheet of what your average pace should be based on your run times throughout Soulcon. We have adjusted for the level of fatigue you're at as well as accounting for running in your boots. But brothers, one lesson we want you to never forget, you should always have brothers in your life pushing you to the pace you should be running in your body, soul, and spirit, and not the pace you feel like running. Please, never forget that lesson. We have built this training evolution around this one point, so you never forget how important it is to have brothers looking into your life, pushing you to the level you are capable of. Which we all know that the level we need to be growing toward is never comfortable, it's always uncomfortable. So adjust your mindsets and find the joy in living a life not called to comfort and committed to sacrifice."

As Bugsly continues my mind begins to run through all of the times in my life when I didn't have anyone pushing me to the pace I was capable of. If I truly am a special forces soldier for Jesus Christ I have to live to honor the King every day and live to love the ones around me with my life. I cannot be a man who hangs his hat on his past accomplishments and then kicks his feet up in comfort…but my flesh wars for that constantly. There have been so many times since I have returned from this Training Center that I have lived on cruise control. Still my pace was good compared to more immature men, and they would even compliment my pace of life in my body, soul, and spirit, just feeding my pride to cause me to run slower. I cannot allow that. I have to have someone pushing me. I commit from this point forward to ask for this type of accountability from my Soulcon brothers in my area when I get back home.

When Bugsly finishes, we all walk over to see our suggested average pace. I let a few of the guys go before me, acting like I'm cool and collected, but I'm actually pretty nervous. Once the guys clear out, my heart rate increases even more as I overhear their conversations. It sounds like the paces are pretty aggressive. So I lean over to read the printed spreadsheet on the wall, and I see my pace, 8:30 per mile. Crap! How in the world do they expect me to do that? I thought he said they factored in the important variables like our sore muscles and these heavy boots. What the heck is going on? I look to the bottom of the page and see these letters in bold on the page:

**If you give 100% effort, focus, and intensity,
you leave no room for doubt.**

Alright, I'm in. I will leave no room for doubt. With Christ in me every challenge before me will be honored and taken with all seriousness.

As I walk back over to the starting line I pray a quick prayer out loud, "Lord forgive me for complaining, and help me learn every lesson You want me to learn in this next challenge. Help me to not believe one lie in my brain."

"Alright brothers, we will go on my mark. Godspeed," Bugsly yells out as he gets ready to run with our team.

"On your mark...Get Set...Go!" he yells out with ruggedness in his voice that sounds like we're about to storm the gates of hell together...

Daily Challenge
Do you have brothers looking into your life that know what you're capable of in Christ? Please hear me, don't give a weak answer with false humility. The truth is you are gifted and created by the King of kings. You are a warrior. You cannot run at the pace you feel like. I understand you're pushing yourself like crazy over this six-weeks, but do you have someone who checks on your correct pace on a weekly basis? If not, don't wait for that person, take time today to ask one of those men in your life to keep you accountable to run the pace you should be running not the one you feel like running. Love you guys, proud of you!

DAY 30

"When I am with those who are weak, I share their weakness, for I want to bring the weak to Christ. Yes, I try to find common ground with everyone, doing everything I can to save some. I do everything to spread the Good News and share in its blessings. Don't you realize that in a race everyone runs, but only one person gets the prize? So run to win! All athletes are disciplined in their training. They do it to win a prize that will fade away, but we do it for an eternal prize. So I run with purpose in every step. I am not just shadowboxing. I discipline my body like an athlete, training it to do what it should. Otherwise, I fear that after preaching to others I myself might be disqualified."

1 Corinthians 9:22-27 (NLT)

As our team starts on this challenge, a surge of motivation is running through my heart and mind thinking about my wife being able to come with me to this Training Center. I can push through any pain for that woman. She has been a warrior wife through so many of my personal challenges, failures, and struggles in my life. I can push to the limit and 10x more for her. I am sure a lot of the guys are feeling the same way, I know for sure Alfred is… I look over to Alfred and reach out my hand for a first bump, he meets me in the middle with a confident head nod. "We've got this brother!" I say as I give a confident head nod back to him.

Without even realizing it, I put myself out in front of the group. In front of Bugsly and the Soulcon graduate who is the ultra marathoner. I look down at my pace tracker on my wrist and see my average pace is way off. I am a little over three miles in and averaging a 7:30 pace. Yikes. I know I have a decision to make, do I push myself or step back to the pace they set for me? I feel good, my breathing is set and on point, I think I am going to press on. I want to see what I am capable of…and maybe I am stronger than I think. I want to be the type of man who truly gives 100% every day of my life. I want this run to teach my soul that, I want to learn the joy in pushing myself to new limits, because I know this body is just a tool to train my mind and emotions to form an unbreakable will in Christ.

After what seems like an eternity, I see a sign approaching, it has to be the finish line. I am still out in front and have managed a 7:40 pace but I am not sure how far I've gone. I haven't seen a marker since mile three. I squint my eyes to see through drops of sweat to make out what the words on the sign say, it has to be the finish. I look closer and see the six-mile marker and I feel like my soul just got completely deflated. My breathing is now completely out of control, my feet are hurting from these boots, and the only thing I want to do is walk. Maybe I pushed myself too hard, maybe I don't have what it takes to finish with a sub eight minute per mile pace – and just then I realize my brain is trying to believe in doubt. "I've got this. I commit this run to you God, and I worship you with my body. I will push when I am in the face of doubt. I will finish strong." I say out loud with as much courage as possible in-between my off-timed gasps to fill my lungs with oxygen. And those words helped focus my mind…praise God.

There it is, the finish line! I look down at my pace tracker, and see a 7:35 minute pace per mile. I am blown away at what my body is capable of when I'm pushed, and I am so grateful! I reach down and pull all the strength I have left, and start sprinting toward the finish line. My body is tense all over and aching in spots I didn't know could ache from running, but I push as hard as I can. As I cross the finish line, I see 53:27, and I finished first on the team… I did it!

As I slow my body down, I walk over to grab some water and cheer my team to victory. My heart is full of the joy of finishing well, and that is a good feeling. I faced this challenge like a warrior. I am actually doing it. I might just become a graduate of the Soulcon Warrior Elite program. I've got to stay focused and take one challenge at a time. But for now, I can celebrate the fact that I just ran at a pace I didn't know I could run. Without these guys I wouldn't have done that, I've got to make sure that I always am surrounded with people pushing me to new levels in Christ with my body, soul, and spirit. I cannot become complacent and I know the decision is up to me. I have to be proactive when I get back home to seek out men that will push me and hold me accountable to the warrior level. I need this more than I know…

Daily Challenge
How can you adjust your schedule to give more effort than you've been giving the Lord? Is there any area? Maybe waking up a little

earlier, maybe sharing the Gospel tracts more, what is it? We know as warriors for Christ faith without works is dead, and we are here to inspire everyone around us to know and experience the life Jesus came to give. So we have to do it. We have to take our lives and turn up the volume. What is that area for you? I challenge you to go before the Lord and ask Him. Maybe you think a fast pace is the one you have set, but maybe, just maybe, you have more in you than you know. Let's push our life to that edge and keep going. Let's find the honor in dying completely exhausted from the Lord's work and with a heart full of honor.

DAY 31

"Then He said to them all, 'If anyone desires to come after Me, let him deny himself, and take up his cross daily, and follow Me. For whoever desires to save his life will lose it, but whoever loses his life for My sake will save it.'"

Luke 9:23-24 (NKJV)

To my surprise, the entire team finished. I was able to meet them each with a high five as they finished their race exhausted. What an incredible feeling.

"Alright brothers, come over here," the Soulcon ultra-marathoner yells out to the team. "I want each of you to take off your pace watches. We are going to hook them up to the computer to see how you did for the goal pace that was set for your run."

Our whole team takes off our watches and hands them over to get our pace checked. As he is connecting each one I am in shock, every person ran faster than the pace that was set for them. Incredible. I stand next to the computer and watch as all of the watches are checked. Sure enough, everyone ran faster than the pace time that was set as a goal for their run. That's pretty inspiring...

"Come over here brothers," Bugsly yells out to the team. "I want to congratulate each of you. You all passed, and you are the first team to pass at 100% on this run. This is a challenge in which we test the heart to see if you truly have the warrior soul. The test that we didn't share with you was to see if you were going to push past the goal set for you, or hit the mark that was expected. Each of you, to our amazement, pushed past the goal we set for you. And let me tell you brothers - that motivates me like crazy. I want every brother in Christ I serve shoulder-to-shoulder with to have the same mindset and actions that you all just showed on this challenge. Men who are willing to go the second mile with more intensity than the first. Men who are willing to see the objective set for them and push past it. When I read, "If anyone forces you to go one mile, go with them two miles." (Matthew 5:41, NKJV), it reminds me of my brotherhood in the special forces. Men who are relentless for their mission, men who have confidence flowing through their veins. And when I became a Christian I didn't see that in the local church until I came through Soulcon for the first time. I saw that same level of intensity in this program and knew I had to be here, to work here, and to spend my life inspiring men to live this lifestyle. I wanted to see men who when given an objective, that would push beyond that with the purpose of honoring the Lord by serving Him with everything they had, and that brothers, is what you showed you have in your hearts today. Well done."

Wow. What encouraging words to hear from such a warrior for the Lord. Maybe, just maybe, I really do have what it takes to live this lifestyle. Maybe I truly am the warrior that I long to be for Christ. Man, I pray the Lord continues to work in me in this way, I hope during these tests and challenges that I find myself to be approved by Him to be used as a warrior until the day my mission on this earth is complete.

Daily Challenge
Share with your team your thoughts about this topic. Ask them how they're doing with their second-mile area of life and then share how you're doing with this. Be completely honest with them, and if you're not where you need to be, repent to the Lord and to your team. Ask the Lord to help you live a second-mile life for His name.

DAY 32

"Then they will see the Son of Man coming in the clouds with great power and glory. And then He will send His angels, and gather together His elect from the four winds, from the farthest part of earth to the farthest part of heaven."

Mark 13:26-27 (NKJV)

Suddenly my heart starts racing and my mind is in utter confusion as I finally realize where I am. I would think after completing a full week of this that my brain would know where I am. But I'm not sure if waking up with eleven other guys to a blaring alarm clock will ever be something that I get used to. I slowly sit up and rub my eyes and realize how sore my body is. I feel like every muscle is sore in a way it's never been before. Maybe after the morning cup of coffee I will get back to enjoying this pain. So I slowly get out of bed and see my brothers doing the same. We have a new rule as Soulcon Warriors to train our wills to be unbreakable in Christ. We can never hit the snooze button, if we do we are making the first decision of the day to get back into our comfort-zones. As warriors for Christ we have to look at every challenge in the ordinary and spectacular as a chance to develop in habits of holiness in Christ. So good-bye snooze buttons. I am in. No more excuses to coddle my flesh.

"Morning brother," Nick says as we head over to the center of the room to pray the Lord's prayer and knock out our morning push-ups. We also use this time to practice reciting our Scripture memorization for this challenge as well as our breath holding challenge. Some of the guys have the breath holding down, but that's something I have to keep practicing. I keep falling about 10 seconds short. But I have a week left and a heart committed to dying before I quit or fail this course.

As we are knocking out our morning routine, I think of the saints who have gone before us cheering us on. To think, right now I am bonding with brothers as we push our lives to the limit and then ten times further to know Christ and make Christ known to this world. With all of the pain and challenges and at times a heart that aches to see my family, I cannot thank God enough for this challenge. What an incredible God we serve. I mean here we are, praying, pushing our bodies to new limits for one purpose, and memorizing Scripture. Amazing. I think of how many men need this. They don't know what incredible things God has in store for their lives. I have to tell them, and I have to live by example.

"Hey team," Caleb says as he breaks through the voices practicing their Scripture memorization. "I want to encourage each of you with a word of prophecy. I believe the Lord has put this on my heart, and I have to share this word of encouragement with you.

I love this guy. He is so bold with his relationship with the Lord and sharing what the Lord is doing in his heart with us. I can't wait to hear what this word is.

"Last night after our team run, I felt the Lord put the word urgent on my heart. As that word struck my heart like an arrow of grace, I had the picture of Jesus on the clouds, returning to this earth. The only thing my heart felt was to share with you guys the level of urgency we have to have on a daily basis. Jesus is coming soon, and we cannot take one day for granted. There are people in our lives that we have to get out of our comfort-zone for, we have to fish for men like we have never fished before, we have to make every excuse possible to tell this world that the King of kings is returning. So I ask you guys, and I pray before the Lord right now, that we keep each other accountable going forward. That we never stop living as valiant warriors, who truly are elite in Christ, who give our all to make more of Him."

"Wow. Amen brother, thank you for sharing. I know I speak for all of us when I say we are in, and we will commit to hold each other accountable to this level of urgent living for the Lord Jesus." I say back to Caleb.

"Amen! Hooyah brothers!" Alfred and a few guys shout out to the team almost in perfect unison.

Daily Challenge
I want you to spend 10 minutes today thinking about the people in your everyday life. The people who, if Jesus returned today, would not be ready. I want you to ask the Lord for a new level of urgency in your heart. A passion that you cannot contain as you think about

the souls that might spend an eternity in hell if they don't know Jesus as Lord and Savior. Ask the Lord to have that passion drive your life. A passion to always be ready to act when the Holy Spirit leads you, a passion that is chomping at the bit to share the Good News with everyone possible.

DAY 33

"And whoever compels you to go one mile, go with him two."
Matthew 5:41 (NKJV)

"Good morning brothers," the Founder says as we all take our seats for our morning lecture. "I hope you all got some quality rest. It's our goal during this training that you realize that earning your time is bed is an important part of living the warrior life in Christ. One of the greatest joys of my day is knowing when my head hits the pillow at night that I left it all on the field for the Kingdom that day. I am not saying that I have the opportunity to do that every day, but I absolutely love the days when I earn a quality night's sleep by pouring out everything the Lord gave me for that day. I hope your bedtime routine starts to look the same."

"I have to tell you, that today is one of my favorite days of this program. We are going to start with our Soulcon test. The only objective to pass this is that you have to beat your original test-in time for Soulcon when you first arrived on the Training Center grounds. Then after that we are going to grab lunch and come back in here for a lecture by a good friend of mine, and a brother who Soulcon links shields with in advancing the Kingdom with force. He is in my opinion, the best men's speaker and best author out there today to inspire men to live the warrior life. You guys are in for a treat. Until then, go hit the restroom, and make sure you have your warm running tops on, it's a little chilly out there this morning."

Wow. Our only goal is to beat our original test-in time? This is going to be cake. This will actually be a resting challenge. I can coast a little on this and keep my body rested for the next challenge they have in store.

Just then I hear Bugsly's voice echo in my heart about living the warrior life and experiencing the joy of exhausting our lives in the second-mile areas of life. Dang. Alright, I'm in. I can't believe that I was literally just thinking that. I am amazed at how my mind will naturally look for the easy way out. I have to continue to push it to live the Spirit-filled life. A life of supernatural thinking and feeling, and not one that looks for the path of least resistance.

"This test-in is going down," Alfred says to me as he pats me on my shoulder. "I am going to surprise myself today. I am going to set a personal record today. No excuses. You in?"

"Yeah brother, I'm in! Thank you for your warrior mindset brother. I literally just had to change my mindset because I wasn't thinking like a warrior, I was looking for a path of less resistance and allowing my body to rest a little. Can you do me a favor Alfred?" I ask him.

"Yeah brother, anything man." He says back as we are both putting double knots in our boots to make sure they don't come untied.

"Can you keep me accountable with pushing myself like this when we get back home? Maybe just a text or email each week to check in? To check to make sure I'm not getting soft and slowly allowing my flesh to have a little lordship over my life?"

"You bet brother. I'm in," Alfred says back.

"Thank you man, that is such a blessing bro. Now let's go out there and set some new personal records." I say as we fist bump and walk over to the starting line.

Daily Challenge
Practice for your test-out today. You are getting close to the end of this challenge, and use today to push your life to the limit. Share the results with your team and focus your mind on finding the joy in pushing your body to new limits. Keep up the great work brothers! I'm proud of you!

DAY 34

"Moreover, when you fast, do not be like the hypocrites, with a sad countenance. For they disfigure their faces that they may appear to men to be fasting. Assuredly, I say to you, they have their reward. But you, when you fast, anoint your head and wash your face, so that you do not appear to men to be fasting, but to your Father who is in the secret place; and your Father who sees in secret will reward you openly."

Matthew 6:16-18 (NKJV)

"We did it!" I yell out to Alfred as we reach for a high five. "I am beat, but we did it brother!"

I can hardly believe that on this freezing cold morning, our team just crushed our old personal records. As my breathing starts to regulate again, I look around at my warrior brothers, all completely fatigued, and honor fills my heart. Almost at the exact same time, the excitement to sit down and eat lunch races through my mind. I know we just had breakfast a few hours ago, but I am extremely hungry. I look forward to what the Training Center has for us today.

Our team slowly regroups and heads into the chow hall to grab lunch. As we walk in, I take a big breath in, looking forward to the smell of food, even egg whites smell good when you're this hungry. To all of our surprise we don't smell anything or see any food out.

"What in the world?" Alfred says to me as he punches me in the arm, almost like he is taking out his frustration on my arm for there not being any food. Then the Founder walks in.

"As you can see there is no lunch and you have entered you next challenge of this course. Facing a 48-hour fast with your team. This fast will start now and we will break the fast the day after tomorrow at lunch. I know you all must be as thrilled as I am, and don't worry, every instructor does it with you. Just focus on enjoying the black coffee, the water, and allow the hunger pangs to be a reminder to pray and not eat. We need more of Jesus and less of this world brothers. Fasting is a great way to train our brains to believe that. You guys all

114

know the heart of Soulcon and how important it is to understand our brain is ours to steward, it can never be our god. Our brain is an idol factory and a lust machine. It will trick us constantly if we leave it to run freely. We have to take every thought captive to the obedience of Christ and force our brain into the submission of the Holy Spirit, and we don't know any better way than fasting to teach our brains this crucial lesson as believers."

Man, this is a bummer. I typically start my fasts in the morning, and most of the time after I have had a big healthy dinner and maybe some nuts right before bed. Then I wake up and have some coffee and get my body ready to rock. I have never started a fast like this, at the peak of being hungry. But praise God, I look forward to passing this test as well and learning from the lessons that will be associated with this pain. I think…

"Alright brothers, grab a cup of coffee, fill up your water bottles and let's head in for one of the best lectures you will receive during our time at Soulcon," the Founder says to our team with way too much excitement in his voice for this moment. I feel like we need more time to mourn that we are about to fast for two days. But I scan the room and it looks like no one is being a sissy on the inside like me, so I man up and press on.

As we grab our coffee and water and head in, I see the guest speaker. Wait a second, is that Cliff Graham? No way, I have read every book he has written. This guy is an animal for the Gospel, but I've only seen a few pictures of him, so I'm not sure. So I grab my seat eager to hear if this is who I think it is.

Daily Challenge
Make sure to start your team fast today before lunch. You will break it on day 36 before lunch. You've got this brothers. Embrace the joys of the pains of fasting and use every hunger pangs as a reminder to pray. Seek the Lord, and ask Him for a fresh filling of His Spirit for you and the loved ones in your life.

DAY 35

"That night was the first time I understood the covering. The covering is the fire. It is the strength, courage, and power Yahweh equips us with. It girds a man's loins when he needs it and lets a man know that Yahweh forgives him when he fails. It snaps our legs when we need it. It speaks Yahweh's wise counsel... It comes only from Yahweh, who alone is the shepherd that we need."

Cliff Graham, Day of War

"My brothers," the Founder says, "first off, I am beyond proud of each of you. You just crushed the last challenge and you are the first team that we have had go through this program where not one person has failed a challenge or quit at this point. Please pat yourself on the back. Keep up this level of intensity for King Jesus! Now do me a huge favor, and get your hearts ready to engage with our next speaker. Like I said before, he is one of the greatest warriors Soulcon is partnered with today. He writes books toward the hearts of warrior men, and he sets up programs to get men immersed in challenging situations to build bonds in Christ that cannot be broken. Recently I had the honor of joining him on an adventure through Israel as we explored the areas of some of the most famous battles, where the ultimate warrior, King Jesus walked, died and rose from the grave. That experience was life changing to see, the words of the Bible truly came to full color in my mind and heart. It was such a blessing! I am excited for him to share with you guys today. Lock your minds and hearts in to the words he is about to share, I know if you listen with 100% intensity, your life as a warrior will be forever impacted. So without further adieu, help me welcome our warrior brother, Cliff Graham."

"You're too kind brothers, thank you. I don't even know how to handle that kind of introduction, I am truly honored. Thank you. I count it a joy to serve Christ alongside this ministry and your instructors. It is encouraging for my heart to see men with the focus of living as warriors for Christ and not passive Christians that live for retirement, and hoping not to offend anyone by sharing the hard Truth of the Word. So keep it up brothers, and I am excited to see how the Lord moves in all of our lives today.

But before we begin, I have to be honest, there is a side of me that wants to pretend like I have false humility and act weak in this moment. It is easy as a speaker to pretend like I don't have a message that will challenge your life to the core, but I have found that speaking and acting with that false humility is just a distraction from the mission I have been given. I believe my mission is clear today and I come to you guys with righteous confidence, the same confidence I believe David had as he sprinted toward Goliath in the Valley of Elah. I pray each of you learns to live with this confidence and walk in it the rest of your stay on this earth. I believe it's possible for all of us to live with the warrior intensity that David had constantly. So please do me a favor, open your heart before the Lord and ask Him to move in your life. It's not my words, or my thoughts that will change you; it's the power and the presence of the Holy Spirit. We are all just stewards of His power, and if we live that way, we will only bring glory and honor to His name, and not receive any praise for ourselves."

Man, this guy speaks with such ferocity for the Lord. I haven't heard a speaker with this level of authority in a while. "Lord, I open my heart to you Sir, and ask that you transform my life today. And Lord, I ask that you help me to have this level of righteous confidence in you Lord. Thank you Sir."

Daily Challenge
As you're fasting today, ask the Lord to fill you with His righteous confidence. Prepare your heart for the message the Lord has for you tomorrow. Come to tomorrow's devotional with a level of expectation that you believe the Lord will completely impact your life. We have to learn as men how to truly hunger and thirst for what the King of kings has for us on a daily basis. Use today to cultivate a heart that is truly hungry for the Lord.

WEEK 05 RESULTS AND REFLECTIONS

Be sure to share your results and encourage others
going through the challenge on the SOULCON App.

Weekly Objectives

- Hand out five Gospel Tracts each week (You can purchase those from Soulcon.com)
- Live the Soulcon lifestyle with food, this time with no carbohydrates after 1 p.m. – Eat healthy for six days, and have one feast day
- Run, walk or crawl, at least two 5ks (some weeks the runs are longer)
    - o These can also be on an elliptical or bike if your knees won't allow you to run.
- Exercise a total of five days each week for at least 30 minutes each time

Daily Objectives

- Start every day on your knees, praying the Lord's Prayer aloud for your family and your Soulcon brothers.
- Knock out 40 push-ups right after the prayer.
    - o Let your Soulcon Dog Tag hit the ground every time. This is a great reminder that falling down is common, but getting back up is what takes the strength. Also, it's a great reminder for your body that it will obey the goals you have and you will not obey the lusts it has.
- Read the daily devotionals
- Drink one gallon of water every day
- No carbohydrates other than from vegetables, berries and sweet potatoes after 1pm (except on your feast day)

DAY 36

"It is a comfort to know that, regardless of our mistakes, the God who loved, forgave, and empowered David does the same for us."

Cliff Graham

"Grab your Bibles brothers, and open up to 1 Chronicles 11:4-7. Today we are going to learn two extremely important lessons about living a warrior life that every man needs to know. Our first lesson comes from this passage of Scripture and there is something you might miss reading through this story that I cannot let you miss. Let's read it together:

And David and all Israel went to Jerusalem, which is Jebus, where the Jebusites were, the inhabitants of the land. But the inhabitants of Jebus said to David, "You shall not come in here!" Nevertheless David took the stronghold of Zion (that is, the City of David). Now David said, "Whoever attacks the Jebusites first shall be chief and captain." And Joab the son of Zeruiah went up first, and became chief. Then David dwelt in the stronghold; therefore they called it the City of David.

1 Chronicles 11:4-7 (NKJV)

"Now let me tell you guys, this story is one of my favorites. The Jebusites thought they had everything locked down as they were situated inside the fortress of Zion. They literally thought their city was impossible to enter from the enemy on the outside. But they forgot who their enemy was. They were fighting one of the fiercest fighting forces the world has known to this point. So when King David gave the word that whoever leads the attack will become the commander-in-chief it was a big deal. This was only the third king in history saying he would delegate this level of authority to the one who leads this attack. So Joab was willing to risk it all to lead this well, and he did. Actually, the Founder and I were recently standing at the opening of the irrigation tunnel Joab made it through. This tunnel was at least 100-yards of mostly underwater swimming for Joab. And it's not like he knew where the end of the tunnel was, no one had ever done what he did before. But Joab did it, risking his life to infiltrate the city and overthrow it. I want you to picture being Joab in that moment, with battle gear and swimming without knowing when he would get air again. There might have been little pockets of air along the way, but that tunnel had to be almost completely full of running water down the mountain of Zion. So not only is it dark and with little to no chance to catch a breath, but there is also water running in the opposite way that he was swimming. That's pretty incredible, right? You know who didn't think that was awesome? The Jebusites. They thought they were in an impenetrable fortress and they underestimated who their enemy was. And I believe this is where most men are today. I believe we have men in the church who think they have lives that are squared away and good to go, lives that they think cannot be infiltrated by the Enemy. Again, the Founder and I were in the spot where Joab made it through, this was a tiny opening that eventually destroyed the entire city. We have to be vigilant brothers, we have to constantly be checking our guard against the Enemy. If we don't, if we think everything is good to go we might forget the intensity of the Enemy trying to get in our lives any way possible. Even the smallest crack, just one small tunnel, if he gets inside our hearts he has a chance to destroy everything, and that is his goal.

"Now, I have committed my entire life to inspiring men to think in this warrior way just like the instructors here at Soulcon. I write historical fiction books based on King David and his mighty men, as well as some of the other Biblical heroes. With this passion, I find myself mediating on the battle we are in as men today. The battle is between following the Lord and being led away into sin and destruction by the Enemy. I want us all to stand against the wiles of the demonic as we storm the gates of hell daily. But I want to leave you with two final areas I want you to meditate on for the remainder of your stay at Warrior Elite training. Open your Bibles up to 2 Samuel 11:1-7. This is one of the hardest few verses for any man to read. The Founder and I were at this spot recently on a trip I led through Israel and we shot a video for Soulcon. We talked about how an entire Kingdom crumbled with this one decision. Let's read it together.

It happened in the spring of the year, at the time when kings go out to battle, that David sent Joab and his servants with him, and all Israel; and they destroyed the people of Ammon and besieged Rabbah. But David remained at Jerusalem.

Then it happened one evening that David arose from his bed and walked on the roof of the king's house. And from the roof he saw a woman bathing, and the woman was very beautiful to behold. So David sent and inquired about the woman. And someone said, "Is this not Bathsheba, the daughter of Eliam, the wife of Uriah the Hittite?" Then David sent messengers, and took her; and she came to him, and he lay with her, for she was cleansed from her impurity; and she returned to her house. And the woman conceived; so she sent and told David, and said, "I am with child."

Then David sent to Joab, saying, "Send me Uriah the Hittite." And Joab sent Uriah to David. When Uriah had come to him, David asked how Joab was doing, and how the people were doing, and how the war prospered. 2 Samuel 11: 1-7 (NKJV)

"This breaks my heart every time I read it. King David was supposed to be out at war with his men, but he remained in Jerusalem. Somehow the Enemy worked a way into David's heart, convincing him that he didn't need to be where he was supposed to be. King David allowed that lie to enter his heart and it destroyed his life.

"Brothers, we cannot let this happen. We have to constantly remain vigilant against the schemes of the Enemy. The Founder and I talk about this a lot, we both believe the only way to live a lifestyle where you're always vigilant is if you have other men in your life who tell you the hard things. The things you don't feel like hearing but you need to hear. Come on brothers, what would David's life have looked like if he had someone in his face, telling him to be where the kings should be? But all we can do is learn from this story and pray we grow more intimate with the Spirit as we learn and apply what we're learning. So my challenge to you is to never underestimate the Enemy, he will always be looking for a way in, even the smallest entry point can completely destroy everything you have. Make sure you have a few guys in your inner circle who will tell you the hard things when you don't want to hear them. Never stop living the warrior life. Thank you for hearing me brothers, hooyah. Finish strong."

"Thank you Cliff, you're a blessing brother! Let's give him a round of applause for sharing with us today." The Founder says to the class, as most of us probably want to not just give Cliff applause, but a standing ovation. That was something I know I needed to hear big time. What a blessing...

"You guys have a break until tonight," the Founder says, "but before you leave make sure to thank Cliff and check out his books and gear. They are some of my favorite books for men out there today. Then I will see you guys at the camp fire tonight."

Daily Challenge
Check out cliffgraham.com He is a ministry partner with Soulcon and a true warrior. As I am writing this I am sitting next to him on our flight back to the states from our 10-day trip to Israel where we actually went to each of these locations and he taught on these principals. I hope you check out his website today. Show him some Soulcon love, and if you haven't read his books I highly recommend them. They are some of my favorite books out there for men. Check them out today! Love you guys! I hope your team fast went great!

DAY 37

"They triumphed over him by the blood of the Lamb and by the word of their testimony; they did not love their lives so much as to shrink from death."

Revelation 12:11 (NIV)

Heading out to the campfire with our team, I can't help but think about Cliff's talk today. It's bone chilling to think that we have an Enemy constantly looking for any entry point possible in our lives. That means like Peter said, we have to remain constantly sober minded and alert. Wow. That was eye opening for me. I need to have men pushing me to a warrior level in Christ regularly in my life or I know I could end up right where David was. I have to remain vigilant, constantly.

"Gather around the fire brothers, and take a seat," Instructor Levi says to the class. "Tonight's challenge is one of my favorites. Tonight we are going to go around the fire and share our testimonies with each other. This is something most men that come through have a hard time communicating clearly from a genuine heart. See, with my testimony, I could make the decision to keep that to myself because it's embarrassing. But if I do that, I make no offensive play toward the Enemy. We have to be men who are constantly playing offense for the Gospel, and when we share our testimony and talk about the blood of Jesus, we overcome the Enemy. And that is a sweet, sweet thing. Honestly, it's something we want men to be doing around the world in churches. So, tonight we are going to go around the fire, and the only kicker is that each guy has 3 minutes or less. If you go longer than 3 minutes it's 40 push-ups, and then you get to try again. This challenge is focused to help you be able to communicate your testimony clearly and concisely when someone asks you. Also, when you get back home we want you to make a video for your social media outlets. We want you to use your phone, or a video camera and record your testimony in three minutes or less, then share it with your friends and family to hear.

"One very important thing before we begin. There will be so many times when the Lord leads you to emphasize different parts of your testimony in different situations. We want you to be led by the Spirit with everything you do in life brothers, we are just wanting to get you to the warrior level with sharing your testimony. We believe getting to this warrior level is done with practice, precision, and most importantly being led by the Lord.

"So, clear your minds, and open your hearts before the Lord. Ask Him to help and guide you. You will notice that your heart rate is increasing a little bit as you think about sharing something as personal as your testimony with a group of men. Allow your body to feel that, but your mind and heart to not be controlled by the waves of emotions associated with this. Stay focused and think clearly. Just communicate from your heart. I will be here timing you to make sure you stay under 3 minutes, if you don't that means push-ups, and you will try again."

As he finishes speaking I think of how long it's been since I have shared my testimony, and I don't think I have ever gotten it below 3 minutes. I feel the flood of emotions start, and I do what Levi said. I remain focused. I must learn this to be able to communicate my story clearly.

Daily Challenge

Make sure that your video testimony challenge is done by tomorrow morning. Just take your phone or video camera, set it on a tripod or a place where it won't be shaky in your hand. Then hit record and share from your heart. You goal is longer than 2 and less than 3 minutes, and then upload it to your social media outlets. Depending on your level of connectedness, you could be sharing your testimony and the blood of the Lamb with a lot of people in one day! Kick butt brothers! Love ya!

DAY 38

"Finally, brothers and sisters, whatever is true, whatever is noble, whatever is right, whatever is pure, whatever is lovely, whatever is admirable—if anything is excellent or praiseworthy—think about such things."

Philippians 4:8 (NIV)

It's hard to believe that our team is still all here. We have been through so much together to this point, and we are the only class to have not failed a challenge to this point. We only have a few days left until graduation, and we just have to stay close to each other and focused on the end goal. The goal of completing this challenge to be more effective men for the Gospel, and the hope that we can all bring our wives back with us for the Soulcon Marriage Training. My wife is going to love it. Until then we have to finish strong. We all have our test-out, our breath-holding test and our reciting our scripture memorization left. It seems like we're all ready to rock, but this breath holding thing is getting some of us pretty freaked-out. We don't know when each test is coming, but we know they are over these last few days.

"Good morning brothers!" Commander Bugsly says to the group.

"Good morning sir," we all say back as a group.

"Today, we're going to test and see if you can pass the breath hold test. I hope you're all ready to go. As you know at Soulcon we are constantly working to find challenges to push you in your body, soul and spirit, with the hopes that when your brain is being tempted you can make the decision to not act based on your feelings, but rather your focus in Christ. This carries over into every area of our lives. We need to know and believe that every day is a day to grow stronger in who we are in Christ, or a day for the Enemy to use our bodies to attempt to slowly destroy our souls. There is no gray area, brothers, and like Cliff Graham shared with us, the Enemy is always looking for any way in to our lives. Therefore, we have to stay guarded and vigilant."

"Who wants to go first?"

"I'll go," my mouth blurts out without even processing what happened. I am just so ready to complete this challenge the words just exploded out of my mouth.

"Alright brother, come up to the front of the class. I will set out the stopwatch and we will be watching to see if you pass. Sit in that chair right across from me, and get comfortable."

"Yes sir," I say as I sit down.

"Ready?" Bugsly asks as he holds the timer in his hands.

I give him a thumbs up, take a deep breath, filling my lungs up with as much oxygen as possible, and he starts the clock.

This is it, I have to pass, I have to stay calm and focused. I can do this. I use my imagination to put me where I go when I meditate with the Lord back home. Standing in a beautiful valley, walking with Him as He encourages me with stories of the saints of old. I love these moments in my mind where I get to spend quality time with the Lord. I work on training my inner ear to listen to Him and to share any anxieties or concerns that I'm facing as a man. It's one of my favorite places I can go to mentally.

"You have 20 seconds left," Bugsly says as he about gives me a heart attack.

I can do this. Stay focused. It seemed like just as he said those words my air went completely out of my lungs. I have been failing this test on my own with 10 seconds left. Crap. Stay focused, go back to your peaceful place with the Lord, you've got this. Yikes, it seems like nothing is working. I can feel my heart rate increasing, all I want is a breath of air.

"10 seconds left brother. Finish strong," Bugsly says as I can barely hear him with all of the panic racing in my mind. Then I think back to the seven-mile run. I pushed on when I thought I couldn't. This is only 10 seconds, I've got this.

"Three... Two... One... Challenge complete. Well done brother!"

Bugsly shouts as I take a huge gasp of air. I did it! I stand up and give Bugsly a big high five. The class comes over to congratulate me. I finished when I honestly didn't think I could. I am starting to believe that I truly am a warrior in the Lord's Kingdom. Praise God for this challenge. I am beyond thankful for this program...

Daily Challenge
Make sure to take your breath holding challenge today. You technically have until the last day of this challenge, but do your best to complete it by today if you haven't already. Focus your mind to rise above the pain and use your imagination to listen to Jesus. All of the mediation practices you learned to this point in Soulcon will help you big time. You've got this brothers. Share your results with your team today.

DAY 39

"Start by doing what is necessary, then what is possible, and suddenly you are doing the impossible."

Francis of Assisi

It's hard to believe that our whole team passed the breath hold test. God is so good! That seemed like an impossibility at the start of this training. I hope the last two challenges have the same 100% success rate.

"Good morning brothers," Commander says to our group. "We only have a few days left, and you each only have two main tests left to pass. And today we knock out one of them. Today is your Soulcon test-out. You guys have been through a lot to this point, and I am sure your bodies are a little fatigued. But you have to beat your test-in time here at warrior elite to be able to pass this challenge. So lace up those boots, and meet me out at the Grinder."

"You ready brother?" Alfred says to me as we lace up our boots.

"I am bro, I just pray we all are."

"I think in this group are some world changers for the Kingdom brother, I believe we're all ready. I hope we're the first class to finish with not failing one challenge. Wouldn't that be awesome?" Alfred says back with an incredible amount of motivation in his voice. It's still hard to believe this is the guy who caused our whole team to walk in our first team run at Soulcon. Now look at him, not fazed by these challenges, and even beyond that, a leader in the motivation for these challenges. Man, I am so thankful for this guy.

"That would be awesome brother, and I completely agree with you. I believe the Enemy is trembling knowing this group is untied together for the Kingdom. The thing he hates the most are men who have wills that are unbreakable in Christ, and souls that understand their need for warrior accountability like this. And as long as we remain with our shields locked together like this, he can't do anything about it. We just have to make sure we do everything we can when we get back home to not lose this brotherhood. Anything from weekly messages, to video conference calls, to different Bible studies together. We have to stay connected at all costs. I know I need it big time."

"Amen brother me too."

"Let's go knock this out. And bring everything we have and then ten times more," I say as we walk up to the Grinder, Bugsly is standing there with his arms crossed and a smile showing all of us he really enjoys this stuff. We all line up in the push-up position, and he starts the timer. Two minutes to knock out as many as possible with push-ups, a little break and then two minutes for max sit-ups, then our 5k. Here we go…

Daily Challenge
Make sure you complete the Soulcon Warrior Elite Test-out. Push it to the limit and share those numbers with your team. You have this entire week to complete this, but make sure you finish it before the end of the challenge. Love you guys! I'm proud of you! Finish strong!

DAY 40

"The one who does what is sinful is of the devil, because the devil has been sinning from the beginning. The reason the Son of God appeared was to destroy the devil's work."

1 John 3:8 (NIV)

My heart is so full of honor, our entire team passed again. We pushed our bodies to new limits and learned how strong our bond is together in the Lord. It was such a cool experience when someone would pass one of the teammates on the 5k. We would all yell Hooyah and keep charging forward. I had the honor to yell it to everyone on the team as I finished in first place and kicked butt. I know it's not about winning, but it's cool to go from a guy who never ran to a guy who is pushing my body to new limits. God is so good.

"Let's gather over here brothers," Instructor Levi yells out to us. "Great job out there! I speak on behalf of all the instructors and say that we are proud of each of you. Seeing you encourage each other on was the biggest victory of that challenge. Well done! As someone whose life was changed by someone looking out for me, I value that above anything else here brothers. We need to know we are not alone. We have, and will continue to have people in our lives that will persecute us and gossip about us, it's imperative that we have warriors by our side constantly cheering us on. I want everyone to go grab lunch and then meet me for our final adventure together before your final challenge before graduation. I'll see you in one hour."

I reach over and put my arms on a few of the guys' shoulders, and we head as a team to go chow down.

"I hope lunch was good! You earned a good meal!" Instructor Levi says as he hands out a card to each of us. "I want each of you to check out these cards. They have five Giants of our time on them that we have labeled. We believe at Soulcon that we have a united mission as warriors. You can see the five Giants are:

1.   Human Trafficking
2.   The Porn Industry

3.   Suicide
4.   Abortion
5.   Divorce

We believe each of these have become giants like the giants of old of the Philistine army during King David's time. And we, like David and his men, have to stand together and start taking a stand against these giants. But these giants, unlike Goliath are not going to die with just one man slinging the stone at them. These giants of our time are only going to fall if each one of us picks up the sword of the Spirit and boldly use it on a daily basis. Brothers, these giants must fall. They are destroying so many lives around the world, and we need warriors like you to take them on. We can no longer be brave, outspoken men in the church walls and sissies out in the world. We have to be warriors in the church and out of the church. We have to be men who long to destroy the work of the Enemy every day of our lives. So we cannot feed any of these industries or ideologies, we have to do what we can to stand in the way of these giants gaining momentum and take a stand boldly for the Truth. We must be the reason these giants are slayed. I want you to meditate on these five giants as we walk up the side of this hill to our rappel point."

Rappel point? Dang. I thought we were done with the crazy stuff since we are so close to the end. I wish he would give us the afternoon off to practice our Scripture memorization. Just then I realize how my flesh is whining like a sissy. "Lord, forgive me for my attitude," I pray quietly. "Help me focus on the challenge at hand with a positive attitude Sir. I love you Lord, thank you for being patient with me. And Lord please help me sling these stones daily. Please use me in this way Lord. Help me be like King David against these giants, laying it all on the line to defend what brings joy to your heart. I love you my King."

As we get to the top of the hill, we start putting on the gear to rappel down the face of this hill, which for the record looks more like a mountain than a cliff. It's a lot higher than I thought.

"This is our final adventure together before you take on the final challenge with Commander and the Founder. The purpose of this challenge is to picture leaving every comfort of this life, and going down into the hells of this earth to live like Jesus. We have so many Christians who think looking pretty on Sunday morning and living in a certain neighborhood is the epitome of Christian living. This couldn't be further from the truth. We need men who thirst for the battle, who thirst to give until it hurts, who thirst to follow Jesus more than the American dream. So as you rappel down this hill I want this to be symbolic of your life. That you are all in. That you will live the humble warrior life for King Jesus and pick up your cross daily. Here is what the Bible says Jesus did for us, we need to do the same for Him:

In your relationships with one another, have the same mindset as Christ Jesus:

Who, being in very nature God, did not consider equality with God something to be used to his own advantage; rather, he made himself nothing by taking the very nature of a servant, being made in human likeness. And being found in appearance as a man, he humbled himself by becoming obedient to death— even death on a cross!

Philippians 2:5-8 (NIV)

The harvest brothers, we know is plentiful, but it's a messy job to collect the harvest. There are going to be hurts along the way, unexplainable deaths, sufferings, but we have to soldier on and do it anyway. When we realize what Christ did for us, we can't help but long to honor Him with the way we live. So, hook yourselves up, and we will go one at a time. Godspeed brothers."

Daily Challenge
This is a challenge I don't want any man to pass up. We ask every Soulcon Warrior to support this global men's ministry at $10 or more a month. We believe this will help us continue to throw stones every day as an army at these giants of our time. The ministry of Soulcon needs your help to reach the highest level, not only with you slinging these stones personally, but with you supporting this ministry as we sling them as well. We would be honored for you to check out soulcon. com/donate and join the Soulcon Support Team. Thank you, I am beyond grateful for you. You are needed on this team. Love ya!

DAY 41

"How lovely is your dwelling place, O Lord of Heaven's Armies. I long, yes, I faint with longing to enter the courts of the Lord. With my whole being, body and soul, I will shout joyfully to the living God."

Psalm 84: 1-2 (NLT)

"We made it brothers, our stuff is packed and we just have to finish with excellence tomorrow then we are Soulcon Warriors. How cool! Rest well and I will see you guys dark and early!" I say to the team, as we all get ready to hit the rack. I am actually going to miss this a little bit. But I have to be honest I can't wait to be sleeping next to my hot wife soon. That is far better than this! But it's been such an enlightening experience for me, and all of us.

"Good night brothers," I say as I turn the lights off and jump into bed, and like most nights here, my head hits the pillow and I am out.

After what seemed like only a few seconds, I hear a loud noise that scares the crap out of me. What in the world was that? Was that a dream? I look around the room and a few other guys are sitting up.

"What on earth was that?" Alfred says with the groggy sleep voice.

"Not sure bro," Nick says back. "What time is it anyway?"

"0230," Caleb says.

Then we all hear it again, "Brrappt…. Brraptt… Brraptt… Brraptt… Brraptt…."

"Bugsly!" I say as we all turn the lights on.

Just then, every instructor runs into our barracks room. "Get up and get dressed. It's cold out there warriors, so grab the right gear. You last day here is going to be a challenging one, but if you pass, you all become Soulcon Warrior Elite graduates… Now what are you waiting for? Get suited up brothers! You have two minutes to be out on the

Grinder."

My mind is spinning and my heart is racing. What could he have planned out for our last day? Doesn't he know we all travel out tonight too? I have a feeling this is going to be brutal.

"Oh yeah, grab your swim trunks," Bugsly yells out to us.

"What the heck?" Caleb yells out, just as pissed as I am. "Are you kidding Bugsly?"

"No sir. Grab your make-up too Caleb since you're acting like such a princess," Bugsly says back as we all get a good laugh.

"Well played," Caleb says back as he laughs along.

We all grab our gear and meet out on the Grinder, ready for whatever challenges are ahead.

"Good morning warriors!" Instructor Levi yells out.

"Good Morning Instructor Levi!" Our team yells back.

"We have a treat for you guys today. We are going to get nice and warm with a team 10k. The entire time we are going to sing cadence, one person at a time. The cadence is going to be our Scripture memory verses. Let's see if you're ready to pass that challenge. And the whole time we're running Commander is going to have his AR-15 and will randomly be firing blanks into the air. We want you all to never forget that every day you wake up into a battle as warriors for Christ, no matter what, so you need to be ready to go on the offense. And in God's word the only weapon of offense we have been given is the sword of the Spirit. So we better be able to speak His Word from our memory when chaos is happening all around us. Stay focused, and sing your verses loud and proud."

I look over at Nick and reach my hand out for a fist bump, he meets me in the middle.

"Let's do this brothers!" I yell to the team as I step out into the spot of the first cadence singer.

As we start running, I sound off, from memory,

Therefore be imitators of God as dear children. And walk in love, as Christ also has loved us and given Himself for us, an offering and a sacrifice to God for a sweet-smelling aroma.

But fornication and all uncleanness or covetousness, let it not even be named among you, as is fitting for saints; neither filthiness, nor foolish talking, nor coarse jesting, which are not fitting, but rather giving of thanks. For this you know, that no fornicator, unclean person, nor covetous man, who is an idolater, has any inheritance in the kingdom of Christ and God. Let no one deceive you with empty words, for because of these things the wrath of God comes upon the sons of disobedience. Therefore do not be partakers with them.

For you were once darkness, but now you are light in the Lord. Walk as children of light (for the fruit of the Spirit is in all goodness, righteousness, and truth), finding out what is acceptable to the Lord. And have no fellowship with the unfruitful works of darkness, but rather expose them. For it is shameful even to speak of those things, which are done by them in secret. But all things that are exposed are made manifest by the light, for whatever makes manifest is light. Therefore He says:

"Awake, you who sleep, Arise from the dead, And Christ will give you light."

See then that you walk circumspectly, not as fools but as wise, redeeming the time, because the days are evil.

Therefore do not be unwise, but understand what the will of the Lord is. And do not be drunk with wine, in which is dissipation; but be filled with the Spirit, speaking to one another in psalms and hymns and spiritual songs, singing and making melody in your heart to the Lord, giving thanks always for all things to God the Father in the name of our Lord Jesus Christ, submitting to one another in the fear of God.

Ephesians 5:1-21 (NKJV)

I did it! I can hardly believe it; I memorized more scripture during this program than I have in my entire life! Wow... I am so thankful for this brotherhood pushing me to give my all for Christ, no matter how uncomfortable it is. Now, I need to focus on finishing this run...

Daily Challenge
Try to sing Ephesians 5:1-21 as a cadence during your 5k run today. Do everything you can to think about, and meditate on Ephesians 5:1-21. We want to be men full of the Spirit, full of God's words and full of passion for the mission we've been given. Keep a laser focus brothers. Proud of you, and finish strong!

DAY 42

"If you want to go fast, go alone. If you want to go far, go together."

African Proverb

Our entire team did it. We all sang the cadence of Scripture that we memorized during our team 10k run! We all even stayed focused while the wild man Commander Bugsly was firing off rounds with his AR-15. God is so good!

"Well done brothers!" Instructor Levi says to our team. "Go grab a cup of coffee then get in your swimsuits. We'll see you guys in the ice bath training room in 10 minutes."

Ice bath training. Don't they realize it feels like an ice bath already out here? At this point I am game for anything, I know we are hours away from being the first team to finish with all of their team members, and then I get to call my wife and let her know that I earned us a spot at the Soulcon Marriage training getaway. Just finish strong…

After we enjoy our coffee we change out, and head over to the ice bath training room. The sun isn't even out yet, it's got to be below freezing outside, and I know this room has the heat on, but it still feels freezing in this room.

"Maybe he's just messing with our minds," Caleb says talking about Bugsly.

"No way, you know this dude is a little crazy. We're going back in this thing," I say back through a shivering jaw.

"Come over here brothers, and get in the middle of the tank," Bugsly yells back as he sips a cup of coffee and has that almost evil looking grin on his face.

We all get in, one foot at a time, then squeal like little kids. Man, Tyler would have a blast with this. I miss that guy. I know he has to be watching us, smiling down. We all link arms to keep warm, and wade out to the middle of the tank, where the ice water is about chest high.

"I told you once already team, if you finish strong alone, you didn't finish strong at all. So once you all say the memory verse together as a team you have finished the program. Then you can get out of there and go into our dry sauna that is only for instructors and warrior elite graduates.

"We've got this guys!" Alfred says. "Let me lead us to the finish line."

"Let's do it brother," I say back.

Alfred then starts and we all chime in reciting our memory verses in unison…

We did it, and on the first attempt! Praise God because I feel like I can't take this water any longer. We all give each other high fives and walk toward the exit, and the dry sauna.

"Well done brothers. Well done." Bugsly says to our team. "You're now Soulcon Warrior Elite Graduates and the first class to graduate with all of their men and not a single failure. Great job! After you warm up, you can get dressed for the airport, and then call your wives and share the news with them. We look forward to having you guys and your wives back soon!"

As we're walking out, Commander is giving us all a fist bump. We did it… We all walk quickly over to the dry sauna and get in. It feels incredible!

Then the door opens, and the Founder walks in, "Warriors, congratulations! I have to be the first one to shake your hands. As each of us reach out to shake his hand, he hands us all a dog tag in the handshake. It was so cool how he had it in the palm of his hand, and then gave it to us in the handshake. We all look at the dog tag with pride, we are now Soulcon Warriors. Praise God.

After we get back and get changed into our clothes to fly back home, we all grab our phones to call our wives.

"Hey babe! I did it, I graduated! And guess what… I won a spot for us to come to the first Soulcon Marriage Training Event here…"

Daily Challenge

Turn the shower on ice cold, and recite Ephesians 5:1-21. Let your team know if you accomplished this challenge, it's not easy at all, push yourself. Either way, make sure you have Ephesians 5:1-21 memorized. If you do, and you have accomplished the objectives for this challenge, you can go to the Soulcon website and purchase your Soulcon Warrior Elite Dog Tag. I'm proud of you! Keep living the Soulcon lifestyle, keep leading in your local church and giving your life to make Jesus known. Now, your challenge is to take a man in your life through the Soulcon Challenge, then through the Soulcon Warrior Elite Challenge. You are a warrior leader… This world needs you to constantly make disciples in the name of Jesus. Love you! Hooyah brother!!

WEEK 06 RESULTS AND REFLECTIONS

Be sure to share your results and encourage others going through the challenge on the SOULCON App.

Weekly Objectives

- Hand out five Gospel Tracts each week (You can purchase those from Soulcon.com)
- Live the Soulcon lifestyle with food, this time with no carbohydrates after 1 p.m. – Eat healthy for six days, and have one feast day
- Run, walk or crawl, at least two 5ks (some weeks the runs are longer)
    - o These can also be on an elliptical or bike if your knees won't allow you to run.
- Exercise a total of five days each week for at least 30 minutes each time

Daily Objectives

- Start every day on your knees, praying the Lord's Prayer aloud for your family and your Soulcon brothers.
- Knock out 40 push-ups right after the prayer.
    - o Let your Soulcon Dog Tag hit the ground every time. This is a great reminder that falling down is common, but getting back up is what takes the strength. Also, it's a great reminder for your body that it will obey the goals you have and you will not obey the lusts it has.
- Read the daily devotionals
- Drink one gallon of water every day
- No carbohydrates other than from vegetables, berries and sweet potatoes after 1pm (except on your feast day)

TRIBUTE TO DAVID VALLERAND

I hope you take the time to read this, and I pray you never forget the words I am going to share with you. I believe it will bless your soul more than you know.

I have to start by sharing that when I wrote Soulcon Challenge, I was full of hope with the impact it would make in men's lives, but I wasn't prepared for the movement it was going to start in the lives of all of us men. I believe the Lord is using the vehicle of Soulcon to truly call and equip special forces soldiers for His army. And I am beyond grateful for that.

But like any of the special forces communities, there are times when you lose men way too soon, and this is what happened with our Soulcon brother David Vallerand. He was a giant among men, and lost his life doing what he was known for, laying his life on the line for another person. If you want to read the article, and I encourage you to do it, just do a search online for David Vallerand in Oklahoma. It will pull up, and it will bless your soul. The death song of a true warrior. I will never forget the morning I woke up and saw a message with the heart-breaking news that David died the night before. My heart sunk. I couldn't believe it. I mean this guy was a beast for the Kingdom... He was a faithful principal in Oklahoma and he was the leader of an incredible family. This guy was a true special forces soldier... I was heart-broken that he had to die so young, and at the same time I was thankful that he got to cross his finish line with such honor. I mean the title of the article in the local news was literally calling him a Good Samaritan.

But I had so many questions racing through my head, and so many emotions. And one that I still haven't shaken off, and I believe I have to share with you guys. It's a mistake I made that I pray I never make again.

You see, I never knew David personally, but he was impacted by my work. He was focused on his health with my first book, Lose 40lbs in

1 Day, then we stepped into the warrior life when Soulcon Challenge released. He would send me emails and messages to update me on his progress, constantly encouraging me on his progress, and the men's progress in the groups he led through Soulcon Challenge. Then one day he sent a message to me and one of my friends in ministry. He wanted to get to know us more and pay for a weekend of hunting for us. And I passed on that opportunity because of the "demands" of my schedule at the time. I didn't realize that I was passing up an opportunity that I would never be able to get back. I often think about how enriched my life would have been if I would have focused more on relationships in that moment than my "schedule." This is a regret I have, and I pray it encourages each of us to not miss opportunities like this. Our schedules will always be slammed, but we might not always have the opportunities to grow in relationship with others. So when presented an opportunity to invest in relationships, bring it before the Lord, don't just check your calendar and answer. Seek to be Spirit led in everything you do. He will help you make sure you don't miss opportunities like the one I missed with our brother David.

In this book I had to honor David's life on a small scale for what he truly deserves in the life of Tyler. My heart was unbelievably heavy writing about Tyler's life. There were times writing where I would have to stop because of the emotions that would come over. I would pray and picture David among the saints cheering me on to finish. I could use my mind's eye to see him telling King David about Soulcon, and having them pray for the work of this ministry together. That encouraged me to press on.

So David, we love you man. We will all press a little harder each day knowing saints like you have gone before us. I pray your life inspires all of us to value relationships more than our daily to-do lists. We love you brother and I can't wait to celebrate with you when I cross my finish line. Until then, Hooyah brother David. Love ya man.

A NOTE TO THE SOULCON WARRIOR ELITE GRADUATE

Congratulations on graduating through one of the most challenging six-week programs for Christian men today. I am so proud of you! Great job pushing yourself to the limit and then ten times further to get to know Christ more and be more equipped to destroy the work of the Enemy! I am honored to have you serving in this war shoulder-to-shoulder with me.

Now here is my challenge to you. I need you to be a leader in your local church for the ministry of Soulcon. Communicate to your leadership team what the ministry of Soulcon offers for local churches. From the Soulcon Global Men's Gatherings on the second Saturday of every month, to the challenge groups, I need you to step up and lead in that area in your church if you're not already. The last thing our pastors need is another project to lead, they need people who will step up and steward the ministries into place in the local church. I challenge you to have that conversation with them, and then encourage them to make Soulcon the men's ministry your church uses on an ongoing basis, then offer to lead the programing there. Soulcon is committed to providing high quality content, soaked in prayer and hopefully the power of the Holy Spirit. The biggest thing we need is warriors on the ground leading in their local churches.

"He told them, 'The harvest is plentiful, but the workers are few. Ask the Lord of the harvest, therefore, to send out workers into his harvest field.'"

Luke 10:2 (NIV)

Let's commit to not leave one man behind. That means we have to do everything possible to bring the men in our churches into discipleship programs.

Also, if you're married get your heart ready for Soulcon Marriage. This next step will be one of the most difficult challenges on the planet for Christian couples. So prepare your heart and be ready to lead with humility and transparency with your wife. I believe your strongest marriage yet is on the horizon, so just keep pressing into the Holy Spirit and continue living in this warrior brotherhood. Don't ever get soft brother. You have to have men pushing you out of your comfort-zone constantly. You are the few, and I'm proud of you. Keep pushing and let's exhaust our lives for Jesus daily.

Hooyah Soulcon Warrior Elite!

Love ya,
Cody Bobay

If by excessive labor, we die before the average age of man, worn out in the Master's service, then glory be to God, we shall have so much less of earth and so much more of Heaven... It is our duty and our privilege to exhaust our lives for Jesus. We are not to be living specimens of men in fine preservation, but living sacrifices, whose lot is to be consumed.

Charles Spurgeon

ABOUT CODY BOBAY

Cody Bobay met Jesus as his Lord and Savior at 18 years old while on Active Duty in the US Navy as a Naval Aircrewman. From that point of salvation to this point in ministry, Cody lives to tell about the Good News of Jesus Christ. Cody and his wife of eleven years, and two kids count it a honor to destroy the work of the Enemy in Jesus Name, daily.

Cody is the author of Soulcon Challenge, Soulcon Warrior Elite and the founder of Soulcon Ministries. He passionately pleas with every Christian man to link together as special forces soldiers for Jesus Christ and advance the Kingdom by force.

Jesus is coming soon.
We have to make the most of every day.